**Psychology zone**

shortcuts to success

# AQA YEAR 2 A-LEVEL Psychology

## BRILLIANT MODEL ANSWERS

### Gender

- Provides the key knowledge and skills for exam success
- All types of questions covered
- Grade A/A* model answers
- Written by examiners

*Do brilliantly in your Psychology exam!*

**Nicholas Alexandros Savva**

psychologyzone.co.uk

**Proven exam success** | **Written by examiners** | Concise, detailed and clearly written model answers

# Brilliant Model Answers

*Published by*

**Educationzone Ltd**

London N21 3YA
United Kingdom

©2021 Educationzone Ltd

All rights reserved. The copyright of all materials in this publication, except where otherwise stated, remains the property of the publisher and the author. No part of this publication may be reproduced, stored in a retrieval system or transmitted, in any form or by any means, for whatever purpose, without the written permission of Educationzone Ltd or under licence from the Copyright Licensing Agency, the 5th Floor, Shackleton House 4 Battle Bridge Lane London SE1 2HX.

Nicholas Savva has asserted his moral rights to be identified as the author of this work in accordance with the

Copyright, Designs and Patents Act 1988.

Any person who commits any unauthorised act in relation to this publication may be liable for criminal prosecution and civil claims for damages.

**British Library Cataloguing in Publication Data:**

A catalogue record for this publication is available from the British Library.

978-1-906468-12-5

**Email us for further information:**

info@psychologyzone.co.uk

**For more information:**
Visit our website for exam questions and answers, teaching resources, books and much more:

www.psychologyzone.co.uk

# Content for Gender

Important information ................................................................................................. 3

Exam skills ............................................................................................................... 4

Specification: Gender ............................................................................................... 7

Sex and gender ........................................................................................................ 8

Androgyny and the Bem Sex Role Inventory ........................................................... 11

The role of chromosomes and hormones ................................................................ 16

Atypical sex chromosome patterns ......................................................................... 21

Cognitive explanations: Kohlberg's Theory ............................................................. 26

Cognitive explanations: Gender schema theory ..................................................... 31

Psychodynamic explanations of gender development ............................................ 36

Social learning explanations of gender development ............................................. 42

Culture and media influences on gender development .......................................... 49

Answers to identification questions ........................................................................ 59

> Please note: this book is not endorsed by or affiliated to the AQA exam board.

# Important information

 *Do not skip this page!*

### ■ Isn't the exam supposed to be unpredictable?

This guide is part of Psychologyzone's *Brilliant Model Answers* series covering A-level Psychology. Use it alongside the Psychologyzone series Brilliant Exam Notes to get the best out of your learning.

This guide to the 'Gender' topic provides a full set of exam-style questions and model answers to help you do well in the exam. After all, your Psychology exam is based on answering questions – what better than to have a book that already has the answers for you?

The exam board has deliberately developed the A-level Psychology specification so that the questions are to some extent 'unpredictable' in order to discourage students from attempting to rote-learn (memorise answers) using pre-prepared questions. This makes it difficult to predict what's going to be asked.

We have tried to make the unpredictable 'predictable'.

There are 86 model answers in this book. We have covered most of the different types of question they can ask you for each topic on the specification. You can adapt the model answers provided to most types of questions set in the exam.

### ■ Some of your model answers seem very long. Why?

Some of the answers are much longer responses than you would need to write in the exam to get top marks. **This is deliberate.** We have written them this way to enable you to have a better understanding of the theories, concepts, studies, and so on. If you do not write as much as we have, don't panic! You don't need all of the content to achieve a good grade.

As you may be using this as a study book, we thought we'd write the model answers in a way that means you can also revise from them, so we sometimes expand on explanations or give an example to help you understand a topic better.

Many of the model answers start by repeating the question; in the real exam you don't need to waste time doing this – just get stuck in!

> Remember: in your exam, your answers will be marked according to how well you demonstrate the set assessment objectives (AOs). We have tried to provide model responses that show you how to meet these AOs. Each example provides you with 'indicative content' – in other words, the response gives you an idea of points you could make to achieve maximum marks. It doesn't mean these are points you must make! The purpose of these model answers is to inspire you and demonstrate the standard required to achieve top marks.

# Exam skills

## How will my answers be assessed?

Your teachers will have explained that your answers in the examination will be assessed on what examiners call **assessment objectives (AO)**. If you can familiarise yourself with these AOs, this will help you write more effective answers and achieve a higher grade in your exam. There are three assessment objectives: **AO1, AO2** and **AO3**.

By now, your teachers should have given you a lot of practice exam questions and techniques for how to answer them. The aim of this book is not to teach you these skills, but to show you how it's done – to model the answers for you.

Just to remind you, below are the AQA assessment objectives:

 **Knowledge and understanding**

Demonstrate knowledge and understanding of scientific ideas, processes, techniques and procedures.

### What does this mean?

The ability to describe psychological theories, concepts, research studies (e.g., aim, procedures, findings and conclusions) and key terms. The exam questions can cover anything that is named on the specification.

### Example

Explain the process of synaptic transmission. [5 marks]

Outline the role of the somatosensory centre in the brain. [3 marks]

 **Application**

Apply knowledge and understanding of scientific ideas, processes, techniques and procedures:
- in a theoretical context
- in a practical context
- when handling qualitative data
- when handling quantitative data.

### What does this mean?

Application questions require you to apply what you have learnt about in Psychology (theories, concepts and studies) to a scenario (situation) often referred to as 'stem' material. A scenario will be a text extract or quote given in the question. You are treated as a psychologist, and you need to explain what is going on in the situation from what you have learnt.

## Example

Chris suffered a stroke to the left hemisphere of his brain, damaging Broca's area and the motor cortex. Using your knowledge of the functions of Broca's area and the motor cortex, describe the problems that Chris is likely to experience. **[4 marks]**

 **AO2 Evaluation**

Analyse, interpret and evaluate scientific information, ideas and evidence, including in relation to issues, to:

- make judgements and reach conclusions
- develop and refine practical design and procedures.

## What does this mean?

Evaluation simply means assessing the 'value' (hence 'evaluation') of a theory or study you have been describing. There are many ways you can evaluate theories or studies. For students, evaluation often takes the form of the strengths and weaknesses of the theory and/or study, but evaluation can also be in a form of 'commentary' (neither strength nor weakness but more in the form of an 'analysis', which is still an evaluation).

## Example

Outline one strength and one limitation of post-mortem examination. **[2 marks + 2 marks]**

## What are the different types of exam questions?

We have grouped the exam questions into four different types:

| | |
|---|---|
| **Identification questions** | Multiple-choice questions, match key words with a definition, tick boxes, or place information in some order or in a box. |
| **Short-response questions** | Questions worth up to 6 marks (1, 2, 3, 4, 5 or 6 marks). These are often questions asking you to 'outline', 'explain', or 'evaluate' a theory or a study. |
| **Application questions** | These require you to apply the psychological knowledge you have learnt (theories, concepts, and studies) to a real-life scenario given in the exam question. |
| **Long-response question** | These questions require longer answers and are worth over 6 marks (8, 12 or 16 marks). The long-response answers found in this book will be mainly for 16 mark questions. |

## How are the model answers structured?

We have tried to structure your learning by breaking down the model answers into four distinct categories:

**Key terms, concepts**, and **theories** that are named on the AQA specification are covered by the identification and short-response questions (e.g. explain what is meant by the term...).

**Research questions** asking you to outline a study, describe a theory or give an evaluation are covered by short-response questions (e.g. briefly outline one study that has...).

**Application questions** require you to apply your knowledge to a made-up scenario (situation) and are covered under application questions.

**Essay questions** 'Outline and evaluate', or 'Discuss'-type questions are covered under long-response questions. Some long-response questions also require the application of knowledge.

# Specification: Gender

## Gender

- Sex and gender. Sex-role stereotypes. Androgyny and measuring androgyny including the Bem Sex Role Inventory.

- The role of chromosomes and hormones (testosterone, oestrogen and oxytocin) in sex and gender. Atypical sex chromosome patterns: Klinefelter's syndrome and Turner's syndrome.

- Cognitive explanations of gender development, Kohlberg's theory, gender identity, gender stability and gender constancy; gender schema theory.

- Psychodynamic explanation of gender development, Freud's psychoanalytic theory, Oedipus complex; Electra complex; identification and internalisation.

- Social learning theory as applied to gender development. The influence of culture and media on gender roles.

- Atypical gender development: gender dysphoria; biological and social explanations for gender dysphoria.

# Sex and gender

## Key terms questions

**Q1** Using an example, explain the term 'sex-role stereotype'. **[3 marks]**

Sex role stereotypes are a set of shared expectations that people within a society or culture hold about what is acceptable behaviour for males and females. This can then be communicated and reinforced by parents, the media, and educational institutions. For example, the idea that males are independent, aggressive, and dominant while females display are dependent, submissive, and domestic are sex role stereotypes.

**Q2** Briefly distinguish between sex and gender. **[3 marks]**

Sex refers to an individual's biological status as either male or female due to their reproductive organs (ovaries, testes), hormones (oestrogen, testosterone) and the chromosomes that determine them. In contrast, gender refers to a person's psychosocial status as either masculine or feminine, a man or a woman. Gender is often determined by the cultural differences expected by society of men and women according to their sex. Moreover, sex is considered to be largely innate while gender is at least partly a social construct and thus is rather fluid.

**Q3** Describe one study into sex-role stereotypes. In your answer refer to what the researcher(s) did and what they found. **[4 marks]**

Smith and Lloyd investigated how adults treat infants based on the sex which they perceive them to be, thereby reinforcing sex-role stereotypes. The infants were dressed in traditionally male or traditionally female outfits, regardless of their sex, and encouraged adults to play with them. They found that infants were treated differently by adults according to what gender they were dressed as. When dressed as boys, they were encouraged to be active and adventurous, and to play with stereotypically masculine toys. When they were dressed as girls, these same children were encouraged to be more passive and to play with more stereotypically feminine toys. This demonstrates how adults communicate and reinforce sex-role stereotypes on children.

# Short response questions

**Q4** Outline research into sex and gender. **[6 marks]**

Research by Imperato-McGinley et al. studied a unique family in the Dominican Republic where four of the children were assigned female at birth and raised as girls, but during puberty, due to hormonal changes, they 'changed' into boys. This was due to a rare intersex disorder in which their male genitalia was concealed, so although they were genotypically male, they appeared phenotypically female until puberty. The researchers found that the boys were able to quickly abandon their female gender identity with few problems, and adjusted to their new roles and expectations with ease. This likely suggests thst gender identity may be quite flexible rather than fixed.

However, the case study of David Reimer proves the opposite. Reimer was biologically male in terms of sex but raised as a girl after a botched circumcision. This difference between his sex and his gender caused great distress even before he was told that he was biologically male, and Reimer ended up transitioning to a male gender identity which matched his original sex shortly after discovering what had happened to him. This suggests that while sex and gender are separate, they can also be deeply related at least in some cases.

# Essay questions

**Q5** Discuss sex-role stereotypes. **[16 marks]**

Sex-role stereotypes are the expectations and pre-conceived ideas of what are 'typical' male and female behaviours. These may change from time to time and between cultures, and are communicated and reinforced in many ways through parents, at school, in the media, and so on. For example, females may be expected to be caring, empathetic, emotional and nurturing, whereas males may be expected to be competitive, ambitious, aggressive and less emotional.

Sex-role stereotypes tend to be developed either through observation, imitation and reinforcement (as is claimed in social learning theory) or through development of cognitive awareness of gender, e.g. through the development of gender constancy (as is seen in Kohlberg's theories), or as part of the process of internalisation (theorised by Freud).

One example of a sex-role stereotype is the widely held belief that women are better at multi-tasking than men. Madhura Ingalhalikar et al. scanned the brains of 949 young men and women in the biggest investigation of its kind to date to test this belief. Using hi-tech diffusion MRI imaging, they mapped the connections between the different parts of the brain in their participants. The researchers discovered that women's brains have far better connections between the left and right sides of the brain, while men's brains display more intense activity within the brain's individual parts, especially the cerebellum which controls motor skills. The conclusion from this was that female brains are hardwired to cope better with several tasks at once whereas male brains are optimised to focus on a single complex task. This may suggest that some sex-role stereotypes are at least in part innate and biologically determined.

However, these brain differences were found in adults, and it is possible that they are a result of nurture rather than nature. It is also worth noting that these are averages, and variations exist within the male and female categories; there will be some women whose brains are more optimised to focus on single complex tasks than some men's.

Supporting evidence of sex-role stereotypes being communicated and reinforced through nurture comes from Smith and Lloyd, who found that infants were treated differently by adults according to what gender they were dressed as. When dressed as boys, they were encouraged to be active and adventurous. When dressed as girls, they were encouraged to be more passive. This shows that adults reinforce sex-role stereotypes on children based on the sex they perceive them to be, which may influence a child's sense of gender.

In addition to this, Renzetti & Curran found that teachers were more likely to praise boys for 'cleverness' and girls for 'neatness', supporting the view that teachers enforce sex-role stereotypes. This was further evidenced by Colley, who found that in secondary schools, pupils had a tendency to view individual subjects as either masculine or feminine. For example, Biology was seen as the most feminine of the sciences, while Chemistry and Physics were perceived as masculine, and this led to girls being more likely to choose to study Biology over other sciences. Both of these studies demonstrate the ways in which sex-role stereotypes can be present in education.

Sex-role stereotypes may hinder an individual's opportunities and their academic and career expectations, as they limit what is considered acceptable for them to pursue based on their sex. As studies show that sex-role stereotypes are communicated and reinforced from infancy and throughout education, this makes it difficult to study which gender-based differences may come from nature and which may come from nurture. This is particularly true for those which are common across cultures or exist worldwide as a result of globalisation.

# Androgyny and the Bem Sex Role Inventory

## Key term questions

**Q6** Explain what is meant by 'androgyny'. [3 marks]

Androgyny in a psychological context refers to a personality type characterised by a mixture of masculine and feminine traits, attitudes or behaviours. For example, this could be a man or woman who is competitive and aggressive at work, but also a caring and sensitive parent. It has been suggested that androgynous individuals are better equipped to adapt to a range of situations or contexts that demand a feminine, masculine or androgynous response, and thus are more psychologically healthy.

**Q7** Explain what is meant by 'Bem Sex Role Inventory'. [4 marks]

The Bem Sex Role Inventory (BSRI) was developed by Sandra Bem. She was aware that society considers some traits masculine and some feminine, but she believed that any person could have both feminine and masculine traits, as these traits exist independently of each other. This means that a person's level of masculinity doesn't determine their level of femininity and vice versa, therefore meaning that people can score high or low on either masculinity or femininity or both. Bem developed the BSRI by asking 100 American undergraduates which personality traits were desirable for men and women, then wittling this list down to 20 masculine (competitiveness and aggression), 20 feminine (gentleness and affectionate) and 20 neutral characteristics as distractors. The BSRI consists of a 7 point scale and respondents rate themselves on this scale for each trait. Their scores are then classified on 2 dimensions: masculinity-femininity and androgyny-undifferentiated.

# Short response questions

**Q8** Outline research into androgyny. [6 marks]

The main piece of research related to psychological androgyny is the Bem Sex Role Index (BSRI), developed by Sandra Bem. She was aware that society considers some traits masculine and some feminine. However, she believed that any person could have both feminine and masculine traits, as these traits exist independently of each other. This means that a person's level of masculinity doesn't determine their level of femininity and vice versa, therefore meaning that people can score high or low on either masculinity or femininity or both. Bem developed the BSRI by asking 100 American undergraduates which personality traits were desirable for men and women, and then wittled down the list to 20 masculine (e.g., competitiveness and aggression), 20 feminine (e.g., gentleness and affectionate) and 20 neutral characteristics. The BSRI consists of a 7 point scale for each item and respondents are asked rate themselves for each item. Their scores are then classified on 2 dimensions: masculinity-femininity and androgyny-undifferentiated.

**Q9** Give one strength of the Bem Sex Role Inventory. [3 marks]

One strength of the Bem Sex Role Inventory (BSRI) is the research supporting it. An example of this comes from Sedney, who found that families with one or more androgynous parent (i.e., those who don't adhere strictly to sex-role stereotypes, such as a mum who repairs the family car or a dad who bakes cookies) have been found to score higher on parental warmth and support. These androgynous parents were also found to be more encouraging of achievement and a sense of self-worth in both their sons and their daughters than more gender-conforming parents.

**Q10** Give two limitations of the Bem Sex Role Inventory. [6 marks]

One weakness of the Bem Sex Role Inventory (BSRI) is that it solely based on questionnaires. Asking people to rate themselves on a questionnaire relies on an individual's understanding of their own personality and behaviour, which they may not have. For example, the BSRI asks if an individual is 'cheerful', which requires an individual to be aware of how their behaviours might be perceived by others and a shared understanding of what constitutes 'cheerfulness'. Paired with this, respondents may want to answer in a way to give the experimenter a favourable opinion of them. This is true both in the fact that men may want to be perceived as more masculine and women as more feminine, and in wanting to be perceived as having traits which they see as desirable or valuable. This phenomenon is known as social desirability bias. Both these issues limit the validity of the BSRI in exploring individual's gender.

Another weakness of the BSRI is that it may suffer from temporal and cultural bias. The BSRI was developed 50 years ago in the USA, and is therefore dependent on how behaviours were perceived then and there. This is both in terms of which behaviours may be perceived as 'healthy' and 'acceptable', and what is perceived as masculine, feminine, or neutral. For instance, the BSRI categorises 'loving children' as a feminine trait, but it is increasingly accepted and encouraged for men to be loving fathers. This is a weakness because it suggests that Bem's scale is made of stereotypical ideas of masculinity and femininity, and thus is an outdated model of personality and cannot accurately measure masculinity, femininity, or androgyny across time or in other cultures.

## Application question

 Patrick works as a head baker in a bakery. As part of a work appraisal he has just completed the Bem Sex Role Inventory. His score shows that he is highly androgynous.

Explain how Patrick's high level of androgyny might be demonstrated in his behaviour at work.
**[4 marks]**

Patrick's high level of androgyny could be conveyed by him enjoying a laugh and a joke with the other men in the workplace while also joining in with more sensitive and intimate discussions. In addition, Patrick may be firm and authoritative with people in his team and also be sensitive and empathic when someone is unwell or stressed. Physically, Patrick could demonstrate androgyny in his behaviour by performing heavy work like lifting sacks of flour while also enjoying more delicate tasks such as cake decorating and intricate pastry work.

## Essay questions

 Discuss the Bem Sex Role Inventory. Refer to evidence in your answer. **[16 marks]**

Androgyny refers to displaying a balance of masculine and feminine characteristics in an individual's personality. For example, this could be a man or woman who is competitive and aggressive at work, but also a caring and sensitive parent.

Sandra Bem devised the Bem Sex Role Inventory (BSRI) as a measure of androgyny as she was aware that society considers some traits masculine and some feminine. However, she believed that any person can have both feminine and masculine traits, as these traits exist independently of each other. This means that a person's level of masculinity doesn't determine their level of femininity and vice versa, therefore people can score high or low on masculinity, femininity, or both.

The BSRI is a questionnaire designed to measure how masculine, feminine, or androgynous a person is. Bem asked 50 male and 50 female students to rate 200 traits for how desirable they were for males or females. From this list, she selected 20 traits which were regarded as desirable for men (e.g. self-reliance, independence, aggressiveness), 20 for women (e.g. warmth, cheerfulness, friendliness), and 20 which were gender-neutral (e.g. honesty, tactfulness, reliability). She then asked over 600 participants to rate themselves on each of the 60 items on a scale of 1 (never true of me) to 7 (always true of me). Although many participants' scores clustered around feminine or masculine, many were fairly androgynous (high scores on both masculine and feminine traits) and some were undifferentiated (low scores on both masculine and feminine traits).

One weakness of the BSRI is that it relies on collecting data through questionnaires. Asking people to rate themselves on a questionnaire relies on an indivudual's understanding of their own personality and behaviour, which they may not have. For example, the BSRI asks if an individual is 'cheerful, which requires an individual to be aware of how their behaviours might be perceived by others and for a shared understanding of what constitutes 'cheerfulness'. Paired with this, respondents may want to answer in a way to give the experimenter a favourable opinion of them. For instance, men may want to be perceived as more masculine and women as more feminine, and people of all genders may want to be perceived as having traits which they see as desirable or valuable. This phenomenon is known as social desirability bias. Both these issues limit the validity of the BSRI in exploring individual's gender identity.

Another weakness of the BSRI is that it may suffer from temporal and cultural bias. The BSRI was developed 50 years ago in the USA, and is therefore dependent on how behaviours were perceived then and there. This is both in terms of which behaviours that may be perceived as 'healthy' and 'acceptable', and what is perceived as masculine, feminine, or neutral. For instance, the BSRI categorises 'loving children' as a feminine trait, but it is increasingly accepted and encouraged for men to be loving fathers. This is a weakness because it suggests that Bem's scale is made of stereotypical ideas of masculinity and femininity, and thus is an outdated model of personality and cannot accurately measure masculinity, femininity, or andrognyny across time or in other cultures.

However there is evidence supporting the reliability and validity of the scale. For example, the BSRI underwent a pilot study with 1,000 students who rated their personality according the masculine, feminine and neutral characteristics, and found that the classification given by the BSRI mostly agreed with the student's own perception of their personality and gender associated with it. This suggests that the BSRI measures what it intends to measure and therefore has high validity. The same occurred when the test was administered one month later, showing a high level of test-retest reliability.

Additional supporting evidence comes from Sedney, who found that families with one or more androgynous parent (i.e. a parent who displays both masculine and feminine traits, such as a mum who repairs the family car or a dad who bakes cookies) have been found score highest on measures of parental warmth and support. These androgynous parents were found to be more encouraging of achievement and self-worth in both their sons and their daughters than more gender-conforming parents, suggesting that Bem's theory of androgyny as a beneficial trait is a valid one.

However, it has been suggested by researchers that gender identity may be too complex to be reduced to a single score and therefore the BSRI is invalid. There are alternatives to the BSRI that have been developed, for example the PAQ which measures expressivity and instrumentality. However, even the PAQ is based on the concept that gender is quantifiable and consistent across cultures and social groups. Golombok and Fivush have claimed that gender identity is a much more wide-reaching concept than is suggested in these questionaires and scales, which suggests that to understand gender identity more holistically and comprehensively, broader issues should be considered rather than specific characteristics as the BSRI does.

# The role of chromosomes and hormones

## Key term questions

**Q13** Identify the chromosomal structure of (i) males; (ii) females. [2 marks]

Males – XY

Females – XX

**Q14** Explain the role of testosterone in sex and gender. [4 marks]

Testosterone is the dominant sex hormone in male endocrine systems. It controls the development of the male sex organs and begins to be produced at around 8 weeks of foetal development when it is switched in by the SRY gene on the Y chromosome. At puberty, increased testosterone triggers the development of secondary sex characteristics such as facial hair and the voice deepening. Testosterone can cause typically masculine behaviors such as aggression and a higher sex drive.

**Q15** Explain the role of oestrogen in sex and gender. [4 marks]

Oestrogen is the dominant sex hormone in female endocrine systems. In the womb, two X chromosomes cause ovaries to develop, which leads to an oestrogen-dominant system. At puberty, it governs the development of secondary sex characteristics such as breast development and menstruation. Oestrogen also causes women to experience heightened emotionality and irritability during their menstrual cycle, which is known as premenstrual tension (PMT).

**Q16** Explain the role of oxytocin in sex and gender. [4 marks]

Oxytocin is a sex hormone which promotes feelings of bonding, contentedness and calming. It is particularly important in breastfeeding as it also promotes lactation so that breastfeeding is possible, and also reduces levels of cortisol, the stress hormone. Women are known to produce more oxytocin than men. It plays an important role in childbirth, as it causes contractions, enables lactation, and assists with mother-child bonding. However, both sexes release equal amounts of oxytocin during sexual intercourse.

# Short response questions

**Q17** Describe the role of chromosomes in sex and gender. **[6 marks]**

The sex of a baby is determined at conception when the sperm and ovum form a zygote (fertilised egg). The sperm and the egg both contribute chromosomes to the zygote, the 23rd pair of which contains DNA instructions to determine the zygote's sex. The ovum can only supply an X chromosome, while the sperm can contribute either an X or a Y chromosome. If the sperm contributes a Y chromosome the zygote will be genetically male (XY), if the sperm contributes an X the zygote will be female (XX). Male and female embryos up to 8 weeks have external genitalia that look the same. At 8 weeks, genetically XY males produce androgens which stimulate the development of male genitalia. In XX females this process does not take place, and so female genitalia develop. These chromosomes also determine whether an individual has an endocrine system which is naturally testosterone-dominant (male) or oestrogen-dominant (female). Chromosomes therefore determine someone's biological sex.

**Q18** Describe the role of hormones in sex and gender. **[6 marks]**

Hormones are chemical substances secreted by glands throughout the body and carried in the bloodstream. The same sex hormones occur in both men and women but differ in amounts and therefore the effect that they have upon different parts of the body.

Important male hormones are called androgens, with testosterone being the most widely known. Testosterone is a sex hormone which is more present in males than females, and affects development and behaviour both before and after birth. Testosterone, when released in the womb at 8 weeks of foetal development, causes the development of male sex organs. Testosterone causes the development of secondary sex characteristics like facial hair during puberty and can also cause typically male behaviours such as aggression and a higher sex drive.

For females, oestrogen is the dominant sex hormone. It governs the development of secondary sexual characteristics and menstruation. Oestrogen causes women to experience heightened emotionality and irritability during their menstrual cycle, which is known as premenstrual tension (PMT).

Lastly, oxytocin is a sex hormone which is present in higher levels in females than males. It promotes feelings of bonding, contentedness and calming. It is particularly important in childbirth as it encourages contractions, in breastfeeding to promote lactation, and in times of stress to reduce the fight-flight response.

**Q19** Give one strength of research into the role hormones in sex and gender. **[3 marks]**

One strength is that there is supporting research for the ides that hormones exert some influence over gender-related behaviours as well as in biological sex development. Van Goozen et al. studied transgender individuals who were undergoing hormone replacement therapy; taking hormones of the opposite sex. Transgender women who were taking oestrogen showed decreases in aggression and visual-spatial skills while transgender men who were taking testosterone showed the opposite. This study design allows researchers to isolate the role of hormones versus the effect of chromosomes, as the transgender women would still have XY chromosomes and the transgender men would still have XX chromosomes. This gives the study a high level of validity.

**Q20** Give two limitations of research into the role hormones in sex and gender. **[6 marks]**

One limitation is that there is contradictory evidence which suggests that hormones have little to no effect on gendered behaviours. Tricker et al. carried out a double-blind study where 43 males were given either a weekly injection of testosterone or a placebo (the control group). It was found that there was no significant differences in aggression between the two groups after a ten-week period. This suggests that levels of testosterone do not directly correlate with – let alone cause – at least one behaviour associated with maleness and masculinity.

Another limitation is that by emphasising the role of hormones on sex and gender, we exaggerate the importance of nature. If it was found that gender was solely down to biology, we would expect to find many more differences in male and female behaviour than there are currently, and for all males (and all females) to be more similar than they are. It would also mean that gender and gendered behaviours would be consistent across all cultures, but a study by Margaret Mead found that this was not the case. She found variety in gendered behaviours in tribes across Papua New Guinea which differ from our Western expectations. In the Arapesh tribe, there were little differences between how men and women behaved. However, in the Tchambuli tribe, women were more dominant and violent while men were more dependent on them. This may prompt other explanations such as the social learning theory to point to the importance of social context when learning our gender identity and roles. This would not only explain cross-cultural differences but also that there are fewer differences between male and female behaviours these days than historically.

**Q21** Describe one study that has investigated the role of hormones in sex and gender. **[3 marks]**

The effects of testosterone in gendered behaviour have been confirmed in non-human animals. Young (1966) gave testosterone to female rats and oestrogen to male rats. He found that they showed reversed sex behaviours, with female rats attempting to mount the males and males presenting themselves to be mounted. This suggests that hormones play a powerful role in gendered behaviour. However, this piece of research may not be applicable to humans as there are key biological differences between the two species. This is particularly true given the fact that human sexuality is more complex and humans, unlike rats, engage in sexual activity for pleasure as well as for procreation.

# Essay questions

**Q22** Discuss the role of chromosomes and/or hormones in sex and gender. Refer to evidence in your answer. **[16 marks]**

Chromosomes play an important role in determining the sex which a baby develops as at conception when the sperm and ovum form a zygote (fertilised egg). The sperm and the egg both contribute chromosomes to the zygote. The 23rd chromosome pair contains DNA instructions to determine the zygote's sex. The ovum can only supply an X chromosome, while the sperm can contribute either an X or a Y chromosome. If the sperm contributes a Y chromosome the zygote will be genetically male (XY), and if the sperm contributes an X then the zygote will be female (XX). Male and female embryos up to 8 weeks have external genitalia that look the same. At 8 weeks, genetically XY males produce androgens which stimulate the development of male genitalia. In XX females this process does not take place, which means that female genitalia develop. Chromosomes themselves are therefore responsible for visual indicators of biological sex, as the genitals which a baby is born with will determine whether they are raised as a boy or a girl. In this regard, chromosomes have an impact on both sex and gender.

However, it is possible for zygotes to develop as intersex. Imperato-McGinley et al. studied a unique family in the Dominican Republic where four of the children were assigned female at birth and raised as girls based on the appearance of their external genitalia – and therefore on assumptions about their chromosomes. However, it was revealed during puberty that their male genitalia was concealed and that they actually had XY chromosomes, meaning that they went through male puberty. This suggests that chromosomes determine sex but do not always fully determine gender, as these children only began identifying and being raised as boys after the hormonal changes during puberty.

In most cases, however, chromosomes (and the external genitalia that develops as a result) and hormones are linked. Someone with XY chromosomes will naturally have more testosterone than oestrogen, while someone with XX chromosomes will naturally have more oestrogen than testosterone. These hormones also play a significant role in sex and gender development. Not only do androgens like testosterone lead to the development of male genitalia in utero, but both testosterone and oestrogen play key roles in developing secondary sex characteristics during puberty. For example, testosterone causes men to grow more body and facial hair and to develop a higher sex drive, while oestrogen causes breast growth and menstrual cycles.

Hormones are also considered by many to be responsible for other gender differences. For instance, more testosterone is thought to cause higher levels of aggression, more physical strength, and a higher sex drive. This is backed by research from Van Goozen et al., who studied transgender individuals who were undergoing hormone replacement therapy; taking hormones of the opposite sex. They found that transgender women who were taking oestrogen showed decreases in aggression and visual-spatial skills while transgender men who were taking testosterone showed the opposite. This suggests that hormones play a significant role in developing gendered traits.

There is further supporting evidence for this from Christina Wang et al. They researched male hypogonadism – a condition which causes a man's testes to fail to produce normal levels of testosterone – by giving 227 hypogonadal men testosterone therapy for 180 days. This improved their sexual function, libido and mood, and increased muscle strength. This indicates that testosterone has a strong influence on sex and gender

The effects of testosterone have also been confirmed in non-human animals. Young (1966) gave testosterone to female rats and oestrogen to male rats, and found that they showed reversed sex behaviours, with female rats attempting to mount the males and males presenting themselves to be mounted. This suggests that hormones play a powerful role in gendered behaviour. However, this piece of research may not be applicable to humans as there are key biological differences between the two species. This is particularly true given the fact that human sexuality is more complex and humans, unlike rats, engage in sexual activity for pleasure as well as for procreation.

There is also contradictory evidence which shows that hormones have little to no effect on gendered behaviours in humans. Tricker et al. carried out a double-blind study where 43 males were given either a weekly injection of testosterone or a placebo (the control group). It was found that there was no significant differences in aggression between the two groups after a ten-week period. This means that the increased aggression in transgender or hypogonadal men seen in the aforementioned studies may actually have been down to the placebo effect or to other factors and the research is not fully conclusive.

Another limitation is that by emphasising the role of hormones on sex and gender, we exaggerate the importance of nature. If it was found that gender identity was solely down to biology, we would expect to find many more differences in male and female behaviour than there are currently, and for all males (and all females) to be more similar than they are. It would also mean that gender and gendered behaviours would be consistent across all cultures, but a study by Margaret Mead found that this was not the case. She found variety in gendered behaviours in tribes across Papua New Guinea which differ from our Western expectations. In the Arapesh tribe, there were little differences between how men and women behaved. However, in the Tchambuli tribe, women were more dominant and violent while men were more dependent on them. This may prompt other explanations such as the social learning theory to point to the importance of social context when learning our gender identity and roles. This would not only explain cross-cultural differences but also that there are fewer differences between male and female behaviours these days than historically.

# Atypical sex chromosome patterns

## Key terms

**Q23** Using an example, explain what is meant by the term 'atypical sex chromosome pattern'.
[3 marks]

Atypical sex chromosomes patterns are any sex chromosome pattern that deviates from the usual XY/XX formation, and this abnormality maifests in a range of physical and psychological symptoms. One example is Klinefelter's syndrome, which affects males and where the individual's genotype has an additional X chromosome (becoming XXY). This can be characterised by breast development, underdeveloped genitals and problems with co-ordination.

**Q24** Outline one atypical sex chromosome pattern.
[6 marks]

Turner's Syndrome is an atypical sex chromosome pattern which occurs in approximately 1 in 5000 females due to the 2nd sex chromosome being partially or completely missing. The individual is referred to as XO and has 45 instead of 46 chromosomes. Physical characteristics associated with this are that the individual has a vagina and womb but does not menstruate due to undeveloped ovaries, is shorter than average, and may present symptoms such as small lower jaw, webbed neck, narrow hips, etc. In addition, psychological characteristics are that the affected individuals have higher than average verbal ability but lower than average spatial ability, visual memory and mathematical skills. They also have difficulty in social adjustment at school and generally have poor relationships with their peers. However, it is unclear whether these poor relationships are directly caused by their atypical sex chromosomes affecting their ability to socialised or because they are perceived or perceive themselves as 'different' and therefore struggle with 'fitting in'.

**Q25** Name and briefly outline one syndrome associated with an atypical sex chromosome pattern.
[3 marks]

A syndrome asocatied with an atypical sex chromosome pattern is Kleinefelter's syndrome which occurs in approximately 1 in 1000 males due an extra X chromosome, making their chromosomal makeup XXY. Despite having two X chromosomes, the Y chromosome means that the infant is still born with male genitals. Individuals with Kleinefelter's syndrome may display poor muscular coordination, infertility from low testosterone, poor language skill, calmness and shyness.

**Q26** Give one difference between males who have Klinefelter's syndrome and males with typical sex chromosome patterns. [1 mark]

A male with Klinefelter's syndrome has XXY chromosomes while a male with typical sex chromosomes will have XY. This means that the male with Klinefelter's has 47 chromosomes instead of the usual 46.

**Q27** Explain why psychologists study individuals with Klinefelter's syndrome. [2 marks]

Psychologists study individuals with Klinefelter's syndrome as they can compare characteristics to those with typical chromosome patterns. This allows them to examine which gender differences may be down to biological nature – as these will be areas in which males with Klinefelter's syndrome differ from other males – and those which may be down to nurture – as these will be areas in which males will be more similar, regardless of whether they have XXY or XY chromosomes.

## Short response questions

**Q28** Give one strength of research into either Klinefelter's syndrome or Turner's syndrome. [3 marks]

One strength is that research into patients with Klinefelter's syndrome and Turner's syndrome has led to the development of therapies to improve the quality and duration of their lives. For example, it is now possible for the stunted growth often seen with Turner's Syndrome to be treated with the application of growth hormones and Klinefelter's Syndrome to be treated with testosterone. This is a strength because it shows that such research into gender – and atypical sex development specifically – is having a positive effect on human experience.

**Q29** Give two limitations of research into either Klinefelter's syndrome or Turner's syndrome. [6 marks]

There is some difficulty in establishing a conclusive cause and effect relationship between the chromosomal pattern and symptoms of Turner's syndrome or Kleinefelter's syndrome. For example, social immaturity observed in females with Turner's syndrome may arise from the fact that they are treated immaturely by the people around them. It is possible that parents, teachers, other adults, and even peers may react to the pre-pubescent appearance of people with Turner's syndrome in a way that encourages immaturity. This is a weakness because it shows that observed psychological and behavioural differences may not be due to nature and it may actually be that environmental and social influences are responsible for the behavioural differences seen in these individuals.

Furthermore, there are issues in quantifiably measuring and making assumptions about behaviours indicative of Klinefleter's syndrome and Turner's syndrome. For example, the idea that individuals with Turner's syndrome are socially immature is based on the idea that there is a typical level of maturity for females, and the idea that individuals with Klinefleter's syndrome are shy and passive is based on the idea that shyness and passivity is not a typical behaviour for a male. But what level of maturity, shyness, or passivity falls outside of the standard, typical, or acceptable range is subjective. A situation could arise when one individual would say that a person is too shy for a typical male yet another individual would judge this person as within the normal range or as not being shy at all. Such subjectivity calls into question the accuracy of the diagnosis of Klinefleter's syndrome and Turner's syndrome, and therefore the research into the psychology and behaviours associated with it.

## Application question

**Q30** Two mothers are talking about their respective children Ben and Dido. One of the children has Turner's syndrome and the other has Klinefelter's syndrome.

Ben's mum says, 'He had problems at school, and there were physical differences too.'

Dido's mum says, 'She did better at schoolwork in some ways than other children. But physically, there will always be noticeable differences.'

Referring to the comments about Ben and Dido, outline Turner's syndrome and Klinefelter's syndrome. **[4 marks]**

Ben is a male who suffers from Klinefelter's syndrome, a chromosomal disorder occurring in males with an extra X chromosome (giving them XXY chromosomes). This can cause both psychological and physical symptoms. Some of these physical symptoms may manifest in the particular school problems mentioned by Ben's mum, which might include problems reading and writing, a tendency to get upset or depressed easily, and passivity compared to other boys, which could make it difficult for him to fit in. In terms of the physical differences referred to by Ben's mum, these might consist of Ben being taller and having longer legs than other boys, having smaller testes, and – depending on his age – Ben lacking facial hair while the other boys are seeing facial hair growth.

Dido is a female who suffers from Turner's syndrome, a chromosomal disorder occurring in females with a missing X chromosome (giving them XO chromosomes). These individuals typically have good language skills and reading ability, which is likely what Dido's mum is referring to in terms of her being 'better at schoolwork in some ways'. However, the 'noticeable differences' she refers to likely include a short stature, no breast development, a shorter neck than other girls, and a lack of mensturation linked to infertility.

# Essay questions

  **Q31** Describe and evaluate research into Klinefelter's syndrome and/or Turner's syndrome.

**[16 marks]**

Atypical sex chromosomes patterns are any sex chromosome pattern that deviates from the usual XY/XX formation. This maifests in a range of physical and psychological symptoms.

Turner's Syndrome occurs in approximately 1 in 5000 females due to the second sex chromosome being partially or completely missing, so that they only have 45 instead of 46 chromosomes. This chromosomal makeup is described as XO. Physical characteristics associated with this are that individuals with the syndrome have a vagina and womb but do not menstruate due to undeveloped ovaries, are shorter than average and may present symptoms such as small lower jaw, webbed neck, and narrow hips. In addition, psychological characteristics are that the affected individuals have higher than average verbal ability but lower than average spatial ability, visual memory and mathematical skills. They also have difficulty in social adjustment at school and generally have poor relationships with their peers.

Another syndrome asocatied with an atypical sex chromosome pattern is Kleinefelter's syndrome which occurs in approximately 1 in 1000 males due an extra X chromosome, giving them an XXY chromosomal makeup. The infant is born with male genitals but may have smaller than average testes. They will likely go on to have poor muscular coordination, and low levels of testosterone which may cause infertility and low or no facial or body hair growth in puberty. In childhood, they will likely have poor language skills to the point that at three years of age, the child may still not talk. At school, their poor language skills affect reading ability. When they are babies, their temperament is described as passive and co-operative. This calmness and shyness remains with them throughout their lives.

One strength is that research into patients with Turner's syndrome and Klinefelter's syndrome has led to the development of therapies to improve the quality and duration of their lives. For example, it is now possible to threat the stunted growth often seen with Turner's syndrome with the application of growth hormones and Klinefelter's syndrome to be treated with testosterone. This is a strength because it shows that such research. gender – and atypical sex development specifically – is having a positive effect on human experience. In addition, such research has allowed for symptoms of these disorders to be effectively treated.

However, there is some difficulty in establishing a conclusive cause and effect relationship between the chromosomal pattern and symptoms of Turner's syndrome and Kleinefelter's syndrome. For example, social immaturity observed in females with Turner's syndrome may arise from the fact that they are treated immaturely by the people around them. Parents, teachers, other adults, and even peers may react to the pre-pubescent appearance of people with Turner's syndrome in a way that encourages. This is a weakness because it shows that observed psychological and behavioural differences may not be due to nature and it may actually be that environmental and social influences are more responsible for the behavioural differences seen in these individuals.

Furthermore, There are issues in quantifiably measuring and making assumptions about behaviours indicative of Klinefleter's syndrome and Turner's syndrome being atypical. For example, the idea that individuals with Turner's syndrome are socially immature is based on the idea that there is a typical level of maturity for females, and the idea that individuals with Klinefleter's syndrome are shy and passive is based on the idea that shyness and passivity is not a typical behaviour for a male. But what level of maturity, shyness, or passivity falls outside of the standard, typical, or acceptable range is subjective. A situation could arise when one individual would say that a person is too shy for a typical male yet another individual would judge this person as within the normal range or as not being shy at all. Such subjectivity calls into question the accuracy of the diagnosis of Klinefleter's syndrome and Turner's syndrome based on behaviour and psychological traits.

# Cognitive explanations: Kohlberg's Theory

## Key term questions

**Q32** Which one of the following best describes Kohlberg's gender stability stage?

Shade **one** box only. **[1 mark]**

a) Knowing what gender you are now and believing that your gender is stable in different contexts and across different situations.

b) Knowing what gender you are now and understanding that you have always been the same gender and will stay the same gender in the future.

c) Knowing what gender you are now but thinking that you were a different gender in the past and could be a different gender in the future.

d) Knowing what gender you are now but wanting to be a different gender at different times and in different situations.

**Q33** In relation to cognitive explanations of gender development, explain what is meant by 'gender identity' and 'gender constancy'. **[3 marks + 3 marks]**

Gender identity is the ability individuals have to identify themselves as male or female. It develops in infants at around age two, when children can identify themselves as boy or girl. At age three, they can identify others as male or female. Children at this stage aren't aware that sex is permanent, which may mean, for instance, a boy saying they want to be a mummy.

Gender constancy refers to the stage at which children come to realise that gender is consistent across situations: e.g. that just because a boy may dress or play like a girl they still remain a boy. This develops at around age six. Gender is now a fixed rather than a fluid category in the child's mind. Once a child has a fully developed and internalised concept of gender at the constancy stage, they will begin to seek out gender appropriate role models to identify with and imitate. This links to the social learning theory, but the SLT states that these processes can occur at any age.

**Q34** Outline Kohlberg's cognitive explanation of gender development. **[6 marks]**

The cognitive-developmental approach emphasises the role of cognitions (how we think) in the process of gender development. As infants grow older, physical changes in the brain mean that they progress from simple to complex, abstract thought about their gender.

Kohlberg proposed that children pass through three stages of gender development between the ages of two and six.

The first of these is gender labelling. Between ages two and three, infants label themselves and others as a boy or girl based on outward appearances such as hairstyle or dress. Children will tend to change gender labels as appearances change. For instance, a boy with long hair might be labelled a girl.

The second stage is gender stability. Around four years of age, children recognise that gender is stable over time, for instance through knowing that boys grow into men, but they do not recognise that gender is consistent across situations. They may believe, for example, that males might change into females if they engage in typically female activities or dress in typically female clothes.

Lastly gender consistency occurs around the age of six, when children come to realise that gender is consistent across situations. They now realise that that just because a boy may dress or play like a girl does not mean that they become girls when engaging in these activitites; they remain a boy. Gender is now a fixed rather than a fluid category in the child's mind.

## Short response questions

**Q35** Explain one strength of Kohlberg's theory of gender development. **[3 marks]**

One strength of Kohlberg's theory is that there is research supporting it. William Damon told children a story about George, a boy who liked to play with dolls, and asked the children to comment on the story. 4-year-olds said it was fine he played with dolls if he wanted to while 6-year-olds thought it was wrong for George to play with dolls. The 6-year-olds had gone beyond understanding what boys and girls do, to developing rules about what they ought to do (gender stereotyping). This supports gender constancy and the formation of rigid stereotypes regarding gender appropriate behaviour at age six.

**Q36** Explain two limitations of Kohlberg's theory of gender development. **[6 marks]**

One limitation of Kohlberg's theory is the notion that gender development occurs as a result of natural processes of maturation. This idea is criticised by social learning theroists due to the evidence suggesting that boys have a much less flexible concept of gender roles and show greater hesistation to engage in activities which are associated with the opposite sex than girls do. These differences are hard to explain from the cognitive developmental theory, because if gender was solely due to maturation, we would expect to find no differences between boys and girls. This may suggest that this less flexibility is due to socialisation and has an environmental origin, rather than being purely driven by nature.

Another weakness of Kolhberg's theory is that through the observation of many children, it has been found that they demonstrate gender-appropriate behaviour before gender constancy is established, undermining the cognitive-developmental theory. Bussey and Bandura found that children as young as 3 or 4 'felt good' about playing with gender-conforming toys and 'felt bad' about the opposite, contradicting Kolhberg's theory. This research better supports the notion that gender may be somewhat biological in nature, or that it is reinforced implicitly or explicitly by adults encouraging and demonstrating gender-conforming behaviour while discouraging or not modelling gender non-conforming behaviour, all of which goes against Kohlberg's theories.

**Q37** Kohlberg's theory of gender development is a cognitive explanation. Explain in what way it is a cognitive explanation. **[2 marks]**

Kohlbergs theory of gender development is viewed as a cognitive-developmental approach as it emphasises the role of cognitions (how we think) in the process of gender development. As infants grow older physical changes in the brain mean we progress from simple to complex, abstract thought, including thought about our gender identity.

## Application questions

**Q38** William is 2 years old. When his grandmother asks him what he would like to be when he grows up, William replies, "I want to be a mummy."

a) What is meant by gender stability? Explain the comment made by William as part of your answer. **[2 marks]**

Gender stability is the stage where children recognise that gender is stable over time but not that gender is consistent across situations. For example, they may recognise the fact that boys grow into men, but believe that males may become female if they engage in typically feminine activities or behaviours. This stage is typically reached at around four years old. William, aged two, has not yet reached the stage of gender stability; had he done so, he would have recognised that he would be a daddy rather than a mummy if he were to grow up to be a parent.

**Q39** Tilly is 5 years old. When her auntie comes to visit, Tilly is shocked to see that her auntie's hair, which was very long, is now very short. When her auntie leaves later that day, Tilly asks her mummy, "Is auntie a man now?"

> b) What is meant by *gender constancy*? Explain the comment made by Tilly as part of your answer. **[2 marks]**

Gender constancy is the stage where children come to realise that gender is consistent across situations. For example, they recognise that just a boy can dress or play like a girl and still remain a boy. Gender is now a fixed rather than a fluid category in the child's mind. Once a child has a fully developed and internalised concept of gender at the constancy stage, they embark upon an active search for evidence which confirms that concept. The tendency towards gender stereotyping begins to emerge at this point, which is typically at around the age of six. Tilly is approaching the stage of gender constancy but has not yet reached it, as she believes that her auntie's gender is altered when her physical appearance becomes closer to what Tilly perceives as male through her having short hair.

## Essay questions

**Q40** Describe and evaluate Kohlberg's explanation of gender development. Refer to evidence in your answer. **[16 marks]**

Kohlberg's theory of gender development is cognitive, meaning that it involves the brain and its processes and ways of thinking. He argues that gender development starts at age two and finishes at age seven, and occurs in 3 qualitatively different stages. Before a child can progress to the next stage there must be brain maturation, meaning that the brain is ready to move on to the next stage.

The first stage in Kohlberg's theory is gender labelling. This happens between the ages of 2 and 3 and involves the child labelling their own and others' genders. Children start to label their own gender correctly and also recognise other people as male or female. This is based on superficial characteristics such as hair length, clothing, or behaviour. At this stage the child doesn't understand their gender is fixed – they believe that they can grow up into the opposite gender and that adopting the appearance or behaviours of a gender are all it takes to become that gender.

The second stage is gender stability, which happens between the ages of 3 and 5. At this stage the child understands their gender is fixed across time and that, for example, they are male now and will naturally continue to be male when they grow up. However they don't understand that gender is fixed across situations, and so may perceive a man with long hair as a woman because they associate long hair with womanhood.

The final stage is gender constancy, and this happens between the ages 5 and 7. At this stage, the child understands gender is fixed across time and across situations and they have a more complex understanding of the permanency of gender. They will also observe models of the same sex to identify gender appropriate behaviours. This is referred to as 'self-socialisation' by Kohlberg.

Kohlberg's theory of gender development it explains the roles of both nature and nurture within gender development – the process of brain maturation is a biological factor and so nature is involved in gender development, and nurture is involved through the child's process of self-socialisation. As a result of this, Kohlberg's theory is more comprehensive and less reductionist than other theories of gender development such as the gender schema theory or purely biological explanations, and so Kohlberg's theory provides a valuable and nuanced insight into the development of gender.

There is also evidence to support Kohlberg's proposal that gender development is an active process. For example, Slaby and Frey found that older children with higher levels of gender constancy paid more attention to same-sex models than younger children with lower levels of gender constancy. This supports Kohlberg's theory that children's understanding of gender differences develops as they age, and that gender concepts develop through the active structuring of the child's social experiences.

However, critics argue that Kohlberg has underestimated children's abilities when it comes to gender. Bussey and Bandura found that children prefer gender-specific toys and want same-sex playmates at age three to four, which is earlier than is accounted for in Kohlberg's theory. This suggests that there may be other factors influencing these children, be that nature, nurture, or both.

Another limitation of Kohlberg's theory is the notion that gender development occurs as a result of natural processes of maturation, which is criticised by social learning theroists. This is because there is evidence to suggest that boys have a much less flexible concept of gender roles and show greater hesitation to engage in activities which are associated with the opposite sex than girls do. These differences are hard to explain from the cognitive developmental theory, because if gender was solely due to maturation, we would expect to find no differences between boys ans girls. This may suggest that this less flexibility is due to socialisation and has an environmental origin, rather than being purely driven by nature.

# Cognitive explanations: Gender schema theory

## Key term questions

**Q41** Using an example, explain what is meant by gender schema theory. **[3 marks]**

A gender schema is an organised set of beliefs and expectations related to gender that are derived from experience, and they guide a person's understanding of their own gender identity. The theory argues that children's understanding of gender increases with age through as these schemas become more developed. For instance, a child may observe women but not men wearing skirts and dresses, and come to understand this as a marker of gender. If they are a girl, they will then show interest in skirts and dresses, while if they are a boy, they will learn that this is not appropriate for their gender.

## Short response questions

**Q42** Outline gender schema theory as an explanation of gender development. **[6 marks]**

A gender schema is an organised set of beliefs and expectations related to gender that are derived from experience, and they guide a person's understanding of their own gender identity. The theory argues that children's understanding of gender increases with age through as these schemas become more developed, and this development of understanding of gender occurs through children seeking out and actively structuring their own learning.

Once a child has established their gender identity (around age two to three), they will then start to search the environment for information that encourages this development of a gender schema. This is in contrast to Kohlberg's view as this process can only occur after progression through all three of his proposed stages. As the child grows older, the schema is able to expand to encompass a wide range of behaviours and traits. For infants, their schemas are likely to be devised around stereotypes as it provides a foundation that can then direct experiences and a child's self-understanding. By six years old, a child has a primarily fixed and stereotypical idea about gender-appropriate activities, and will disregard information that doesn't fit with their existing schema.

Children will also, importantly, have a better understanding of schemas appropriate to their own gender because they will pay more attention to information associated with their own gender identiy. However, around age eight, this will shift and children will develop elaborate schemas for both genders. They will often then enforce these standards on their peers.

**Q43** Explain one strength of gender schema theory of gender development. **[3 marks]**

A strength of the gender scheme theory comes from research evidence supporting it. A study conducted by Martin and Halverson (1983) found that children were more likely to remember photographs of gender-consistent behaviour (e.g. a male firefighter) than inconsistent (e.g. a female firefighter), and they often misremembered the picture, saying that the firefighter was male when they were female. This supports the predictions of gender schema theory, which states that children will disregard information which does not match their gender schemas.

**Q44** Explain one limitation of the gender schema theory of gender development. **[3 marks]**

A limitation of gender schema theory is that it is probable that the importance of schemas and other cognitive concepts are exaggerated in this theory. As with Kohlberg's theory, it is possible that this theory doesn't pay sufficient attention to the effect that rewards and punishments that a child receives can have on their gendered behaviour. For example, if a boy is playing with trucks and is told they're a good boy, they're more likely to do it again. But if a girl is scolded for playing with trucks, it is unlikely they'll do it again in the future. Likewise, if a boy is told that dolls are for girls by their peers and mocked for playing with them, they are unlikely to want to engage in behaviours that will see them socially ostricised. Meanwhile, a girl may choose to play with dolls for the rewards associated with socialising with her peers rather than because her own gender schema says she should. Whether a child is rewarded or punished will shape behaviour and is likely to encourage the development of gender-stereotyped behaviours in children, which gender schema theory does not acknowledge.

**Q45** Explain one difference between Kohlberg's theory of gender development and gender schema theory. **[3 marks]**

Martin and Halverson suggest that gender schemas are an outcome of children actively structuring their own experiences, rather than passive learning through observing and imitating, as Kohlberg suggests in his theory of gender development. Unlike Kohlberg, they believe that children start learning about gender-appropriate behaviour before gender constancy is achieved, claiming that basic gender identity (gender labelling) is sufficient for a child to identify as a boy or a girl and take an interest in behaviours that are appropriate based on that identity.

**Q46** Describe one study that has investigated gender schema theory. **[6 marks]**

Liben and Signorella (1993) showed 106 primary school children sixty drawings of male and female characters engaged in masculine, feminine, and neutral activities or occupations (e.g. as a firefighter, washing dishes), and then asked them to recall as many of the pictures as possible. The results indicated that children recalled more pictures of men performing masculine behaviors than of men performing feminine behaviors. They concluded that the influence of gender schemas can be so strong that counter stereotypical information may be distorted or discarded to make it fit in with the schemas. However, it can be argued that the study of children can bring about methodological issues as they are more subject to demand characterises, giving answers they think will please the researcher, therefore lowering the internal validity of the study.

## Application questions

**Q47** As part of a study into gender schemas, an opportunity sample of 50 boys aged 6 years from a primary school watched a film. In the film, a man was seen watching TV, mowing the lawn and doing the ironing.

One week later, all the boys were asked to recall what they had seen in the film.

The results are shown in the table below.

Number of boys who recalled each activity shown in the film

| Activity shown in the film | Number of boys who recalled seeing the activity |
|---|---|
| Man watching TV | 47 |
| Man mowing the lawn | 49 |
| Man doing the ironing | 23 |

Use your knowledge of gender schema theory to explain the results shown in the table above.
**[4 marks]**

The results indicate that the recall of the activities of watching TV and mowing the lawn was almost perfect or otherwise extremely high, but recall for ironing was only 23/50, just less than half. This is likely due to the gender schemas which the participants have. Gender schemas are a formation of stereotypes and expectations about what certain genders do; in this case, it is likely that watching TV is seen as a neutral activity, mowing the lawn is seen as masculine, and ironing is seen as feminine. This is because men are, on average, more likely to mow the lawn while women are more likely to do the ironing, which contributes to the boys' gender schemas about what men and women do. Gender schema theory proposes that children are likely to discard or distort information which doesn't fit their schemas, which this research supports, as the gender non-conforming behaviour was most likely to be forgotten by the children.

**Q48** Beatrix is three years old. At her nursery, there are lots of toys to play with but Beatrix nearly always chooses to play with the dolls and the toy kitchen. When she comes home from nursery she tells her mother about other girls at nursery but hardly ever mentions any of the boys.

Use your knowledge of gender schema theory to explain Beatrix's behaviour at nursery and at home. **[4 marks]**

Beatrix is three years old so will have developed a gender identity of herself as a girl, and along with that, is developing a 'girl' schema. Her 'girl' schema is an organised group of concepts which consists of all the knowledge she has of girls and how they look and behave. This will be why she plays with traditionally feminine toys at nursery; her schema tells her that this is the right behaviour for her. At home, Beatrix talks mainly about what the girls have been doing as she pays more attention to their behaviour, which happens because she is actively trying to expand her girl schema or in-group knowledge. Beatrix talks rarely about what boys do because this information is not yet relevant to her; she will develop her schema about what boys do when she is an older child.

# Essay questions

**Q49** Discuss gender schema as an explanations of gender development. **[16 marks]**

At the core of the gender schema theory is the notion of 'schema': a mental representation that guides the processing of information and experiences. Gender schemas expand to include a wide range of behaviours and personality traits which are appropriate and normal for a specific gender. For young children, schema are likely to be formed around stereotypes, such as boys play with trucks and girls play with dolls, and these provide a framework that directs experience and self-understanding. Martin and Halverson suggest that gender identity is developed through children actively seeking out knowledge and structuring their own experiences to develop these schemas, and that they will develop the schema for their own gender in more detail before they develop the schema for the opposite gender.

The first schema consists of two categories: boy/girl. The child's own sex is considered the in-group while the opposite sex is considered the out-group. Once a child identifies with their gender, they think of others of that gender as an in-group, and those who are 'different' (i.e. don't share their gender) as an out-group. This identification leads them to emulate in-group behaviors and avoid out-group behaviors. Children will actively seek out information about what their in-group does to try to acquire schemas of understanding relating to gender-appropriate behavior. This can lead to conclusions like 'boys shouldn't have long hair', 'boys like trucks' or 'it is wrong for boys to cry.

Elements of gender schema theory are backed by research, supporting its validity as a concept. Liben and Signorella (1993) showed 106 primary school children sixty drawings of male and female characters engaged in masculine, feminine, and neutral activities or occupations (e.g. as a firefighter, washing dishes), and then asked them to recall as many of the pictures as possible. The results indicated that children recalled more pictures of men performing masculine behaviors than of men performing feminine behaviors. They concluded that the influence of gender schemas can be so strong that counter stereotypical information may be distorted or discarded to make it fit in with the schemas.

However, it is possible that this is down to other factors and does not fully validate the theory. For instance, it may be that these children had not reached the stage which Kohlberg describes in his theory of gender development as gender constancy. At this stage, a child understands that gender is fixed across time and across situations, but children who have not yet reached this stage may see men performing feminine behaviours as not being men. This alternate explanation for the research findings means that it cannot be definitive proof of gender schema theory as a concept.

Arguably, gender schema theory and Kohlberg's theory can be seen as complementary, rather than polar opposites. For example, Kohlberg's theory may explain the process of children acquiring motivation to confirm their gender identity, after reaching the stage of gender constancy, through seeking out experiences and role models which are gender-consistent. On the other hand, gender schema theory may describe a different process where such schemas distort the memory and perception of a child as to what is gender-consistent, to be followed up by Kohlberg's stages.

A limitation of both of these theories, even when applied simultaneously, is that it is probable that the importance of schemas and other cognitive concepts are exaggerated. It is possible that this theory doesn't pay sufficient attention to the role of societal factors such as parental influence and the effect that rewards and punishments that a child receives can have on their gendered behaviour. For example, if a boy is playing with trucks and is told they're a good boy, they're more likely to do it again. But if a girl is scolded for playing with trucks, it is unlikely they'll do it again in the future. Likewise, if a boy is told that dolls are for girls by their peers and mocked for playing with them, they are unlikely to want to engage in behaviours that will see them socially ostricised. Meanwhile, a girl may choose to play with dolls for the rewards associated with socialising with her peers rather than because her own gender schema says she should. Whether a child is rewarded or punished will shape behaviour and is likely to encourage the development of gender-stereotyped behaviours in children, which gender schema theory does not adequately acknowledge. Because of this, the theory can't really explain how gender schemas develop and take the shape they do.

A further limitation of gender schema theory is its emphasis on the importance of parents and peers in the formation and maintenance of a schema ignores the role of nurture. Alternate biological explanations suggest that gendered behaviour is due to innate processes resulting in instinctual behaviour that isn't dependent on schemas. This is supported by the fact that gendered behaviours are also seen in animals; for instance, a study by Young found that injecting female rats with testosterone caused them to behave in a more masculine way, and injecting male rats with oestrogen made their behaviour more feminine. If these gendered behaviours were solely down to schemas, hormones would have had no impact. Because there seems to be evidence for both approaches and therefore a biosocial approach to gender is popular to weigh up the differences in the nature and nurture debate.

# Psychodynamic explanations of gender development

## Key term questions

**Q50** According to psychoanalytic theory, which two of A, B, C, D, and E have a very important role in gender development?

Shade **two** boxes only. [2 marks]

    A. Identification
    B. Imitation
    C. Initiation
    D. Internalisation
    E. Interpretation

**Q51** Which one of the following statements about Freud's psychoanalytic theory of gender development is false?

Shade **one** box only. [1 mark]

Freud suggests that little boys

    A. are afraid of their father.
    B. are jealous of their father.
    C. are jealous of their mother.
    D. come to internalise their father's views.
    E. have a romantic attachment to their mother.

**Q52** With reference to Freud's psychodynamic theory of gender development, explain what is meant by 'identification' and 'internalisation' [4 marks]

Identification is a concept whereby a person adopts a set of attitudes or behaviours due to a desire to associate with a particular person or group. This is important in gender development as, through the resolution of the Oedipus and Electra complexes, the child comes to identify with their same-sex parent. Internalisation occurs when a person accepts these attitudes and behaviour as their own. When children identify with their same-sex parent, they internalise their shared gender, thus receiving a 'second-hand' gender identity.

**Q53** With reference to Freud's psychodynamic theory of gender development, explain what is meant by 'Oedipus complex'. **[4 marks]**

During the phallic stage, boys develop what Freud refers to as the Oedipus complex. This is where they will develop incestuous feelings towards their mother and hold a jealous and murderous hatred for their father, who they see as standing in the way of the mother's love. However, the boy also realises that the father is more powerful than he is, and he fears that he may be castrated by his father, which is known as castration anxiety. In order to resolve this conflict, the boy gives up his love for his mother, and begins to identify with the father, which Freud refers to as identification with the aggressor. This leads to the internalisation of a male gender identity.

**Q54** With reference to Freud's psychodynamic theory of gender development, explain what is meant by 'Electra complex' **[4 marks]**

During the phallic stage, girls will develop what neo-Freudian psychologist Carl Jung refers to as the Electra complex. This is where they experience penis envy and see their mother as competition for their father's love. As a result of this, girls develop a double-resentment, one as they see the mother as a love rival and one blaming their mother for their lack of penis. However, over time, girls come to accept that they will never have a penis, and substitute this envy for the desire to have children. Furthermore, they realise that they don't want to lose their mother's love over their father, and so repress these feelings, identifying with the mother as a result. This leads to the internalisation of a female gender identity.

## Short response questions

**Q55** Outline Freud's psychodynamic theory of gender development. **[6 marks]**

Freud's psychodynamic theory explains how gender development occurs during the phallic stage of development. Prior to this phase, children have no concept of gender identity, with Freud often descriving them as 'bisexual', in this case meaning that they are neither masculine nor feminine. However, during the phallic stage, the focus of pleasure switches to the genitals and children experience either the Oedipus or the Electra complex based on their sex, which is critical to the formation of their gender identity.

The Oedipus complex is where boys will develop incestuous feelings towards their mother and hold a jealous and murderous hatred for their father, who they see as standing in the way of the mother's love. However, the boy also realises that the father is more powerful than he is, and he fears he may be castrated by his father, which is known as castration anxiety. In order to resolve this conflict, the boy gives up his love for his mother, and begins to identify with the father, which Freud refers to as identification with the aggressor.

The Electra complex is where girls will experience two key things. The first is penis envy and the second is perceiving their mother as competition for their father's love. As a result of this, girls develop a double-resentment of their mother as both a love rival and the person to blame for their lack of penis. However, over time, girls come to accept that they will never have a penis, and substitute this envy for the desire to have children. Furthermore, they realise that they don't want to lose their mother's love over their father, and so repress these feelings, identifying with the mother as a result.

The critical element is that children of both sexes identify with their same-sex parent to resolve their complex, and thus internalise the gender identity of that parent. This cements their own gender identity in place.

**Q56** Give one strength of Freud's psychodynamic theory of gender development. **[3 marks]**

One strength of Freud's psychodynamic theory of gender development is that there is supporting research evidence from Freud's own case study of Little Hans. Hans was a five year old boy, entering the phallic stage of development. He developed sexual feelings for his mother and expressed a murderous hatred for his father; this lead to the development of castration anxiety as a theory. However, in Hans' case, he had transferred his fear of his father onto horses via displacement. Freud determined that his theories were true as the anxiety Hans experienced was resolved when he finally identified with his father.

**Q57** Give one limitations of Freud's psychodynamic theory of gender development. **[6 marks]**

One limitation is that some critics believe Freud's psychodynamic theories are too much of a product of their time and reflect the age's socio-cultural biases. While Freud wrote in great detail about the Oedipus complex, the parallel for girls was actually theorised by Carl Jung, one of Freud's colleagues. Freud openly admitted that women were of a mystery to him, and this notion of penis envy has been criticised for reflecting the patriatchal Victorian era within which he lived in. Horney, a feminist psychoanalyst, suggested that a more overwhelming emotion than penis envy is the male experience of 'womb envy,' resulting from a man's lack of ability to nurture and sustain life. Further to this, she challenged the idea of penis envy, suggesting it was a cultural concept, and that the theory presented for female gender development was founded on androcentric assumptions.

**Q58** Describe one study that has investigated Freud's psychodynamic theory of gender development. **[4 marks]**

One study that investigated Freud's theory was the case study of Little Hans, conducted by Freud himself. Hans was a five year old boy, at the phallic stage of development where he developed sexual feelings for his mother and a murderous hatred for his father, leading to castration anxiety. This repressed fear of castration was expressed through a fear of horses. However, this fear was overcome and Hans's anxiety was resolved when he came to identify with his father. This suggests that through resolving the Oedipus complex, his anxiety also dissipated as he internalised his father's gender identity and thus not longer felt castration anxiety.

## Application question

 Joey has stolen a bag of sweets from the local shop. His friend Ross says: "My dad says that stealing is wrong and I agree with him."

With reference to the Oedipus complex, explain why Ross agrees with his father. **[2 marks]**

Ross has internalised his father's morals and values as a result of resolving his Oedipus complex, meaning he does not see his father as an aggressor looking to castrate him or compete with him for his mother's love, but instead identifies with him.

## Essay questions

 Outline and briefly discuss Freud's theory of the Oedipus complex as an explanation for gender development in boys. **[8 marks]**

Freud's psychodynamic theory explains how gender development occurs during the phallic stage. Prior to this phase, children have no concept of gender identity, with Freud often descriving them as 'bisexual', in this case meaning that they are neither masculine nor feminine. However, during the phallic stage, the focus of pleasure switches to the genitals and children experience the Oedipus or Electra complex based on their sex, which is critical to gender identity. The Oedipus complex is only experienced by males.

The Oedipus complex is where boys will develop incestuous feelings towards their mother and hold a jealous and murderous hatred for their father, who they see as standing in the way of the mother's love. However, the boy also realises that the father is more powerful than he is, and he fears he may be castrated by his father, which is known as castration anxiety. In order to resolve this conflict, the boy gives up his love for his mother, and begins to identify with the father, which Freud refers to as identification with the aggressor. The critical element is that boys identify with their father as their same-sex parent in order to resolve their complex and thus internalise a male gender identity.

Freud presented the case study of Little Hans to support his theory. Hans was a young boy who had a fear of horses biting him, which Freud saw as representing castration anxiety. As this fear resolved itself when Hans started identifying more with his father, Freud determined that these things are linked and that the fear was an example of displacement.

However, the Oedipus complex is unconscious and it is impossible to falsify. It cannot be tested or reliably proved, and this makes it an unscientific explanation for gender development. There is also contradictory evidence as Freud's theory suggests that boys with strict fathers would go on to develop a stronger sense of gender identity because they would suffer more castration anxiety, and therefore eventually identify more strongly with their father when their Oedipus complex is resolved. However, Blakemore and Hill found that boys with more liberal fathers are likely to be more secure in their masculine identity, which does not fit with Freud's theory of gender development.

In addition, Freud's theory is only applicable to boys who grew up in a nuclear family. However, many boys grow up in single-parent families, have parents of the same gender, or are otherwise raised in a non-nuclear family environment. There is no research evidence that this detrimentally affects their gender development, which challenges the validity of Freud's theories.

**Q61** Discuss Freud's psychodynamic theory of gender development. **[16 marks]**

Freud's psychodynamic theory explains how gender development occurs during the phallic stage. Prior to this phase, children have no concept of gender identity, with Freud describing them as 'bisexual', in this case meaning that they are neither masculine nor feminine. However, during the phallic stage, the focus of pleasure switches to the genitals and children experience the Oedipus or Electra complex, and this is critical to the development of their gender identity.

The Oedipus complex is where boys will develop incestuous feelings towards their mother and hold a jealous and murderous hatred for their father, who they see as standing in the way of the mother's love. However, the boy also realises that the father is more powerful than he is, and he fears he may be castrated by his father, which is known as castration anxiety. In order to resolve this conflict, the boy gives up his love for his mother, and begins to identify with the father, which Freud refers to as identification with the aggressor.

The Electra complex is where girls will experience two key things. The first is penis envy and the second is perceiving their mother as competition for their father's love. As a result of this, girls develop a double-resentment as both a love rival and the person to blame for their lack of penis. However, over time, girls come to accept that they will never have a penis, and substitute this envy for the desire to have children. Furthermore, they realise that they don't want to lose their mother's love over their father, and so repress these feelings, identifying with the mother as a result.

The critical element is that children of both sexes identify with their same-sex parent to resolve their complex and thus internalise the gender identity of that parent. This cements their own gender identity in place.

Freud supported his theory with a case study of Little Hans. Hans was a five year old boy, entering the phallic stage of development. He developed sexual feelings for his mother and expressed a murderous hatred for his father, which lead to the development of castration anxiety. However, in Hans' case, he had transferred his fear of his father onto horses via displacement. His anxiety was resolved when he finally identified with his father, which suggests that Freud's theory on the cause of his anxiety has some truth to it.

However, while Freud wrote in great detail about the Oedipus complex, the parallel for girls was actually theorised by Carl Jung, one of Freud's colleagues. Freud openly admitted that women were of a mystery to him, and this notion of penis envy has been criticised for reflecting the patriatchal Victorian era within which he lived in. Horney, a feminist psychoanalyst suggested that a more overwhelming emotion than penis envy is the male experience of 'womb envy,' resulting from a man's lack of ability to nurture and sustain life. Further to this, she challenged the idea of penis envy, suggesting it was a cultural concept, and that the psychodynamic theories on female gender development were founded on androcentric assumptions. It is possible that psychodynamic explanations of gender development are a product of their time and reflect the age's socio-cultural biases, and therefore lacks temporal validity.

Furthermore, paired with this potential androcentricism, it has also been criticised for being unscientific. This is because many of the concepts Freud refers to in his theory of gender development are unconscious and therefore untestable. This provides a stark contrast to other explanation of gender such as those based on hormonal factors that are based on objective evidence from controlled lab experiments. According to Popper, because Freud's theory can't be tested, it means his key ideas can't be falsified, and thus makes his theory pseudoscientific.

In addition, Freudian theory is only applicable to children who grew up in a nuclear family, as both the Oedipus and Electra complexes require both a same-sex and opposite-sex parent to be the only main caregivers. However, many boys grow up in single-parent families, have parents of the same gender, or are otherwise raised in a non-nuclear family environment. There is no research evidence that this detrimentally affects their gender development, which challenges the validity of Freud's theories. In fact, Golombok et al. showed that children from single parent-families went on to develop normal gender identities, even when the parent and child were of opposite genders.

# Social learning explanations of gender development

## Short response questions

**Q62** Outline social learning theory as applied to gender development. **[6 marks]**

The social learning theory of gender development states that our gendered behaviour is learnt through observing others. It draws attention to the influence of nurture and the way our environment shapes gender development.

Before a child starts observing others, they will first undergo identification. This refers to the process by which a child 'attaches' themselves to a person who is seen to be 'like them' and who has qualities the child admires. These individuals are known as role models and they may be part of a child's immediate environment or present within media. Modelling is the precise demonstration of a behaviour that may be imitated by an observer, and this imitation occurs when a child identifies with a role model. For example, a mother may make dinner and set the table (stereotypical behaviour) and her daughter will go on to imitate this in her play.

The process by which they observe and imitate this gendered behaviour is known as mediational processes. According to Bandura, there are four elements that lead to the behaviours taking place. The first is attention, in which the child observes and notices the behaviour of their role model. The second is retention, in which they code and store this knowledge into their long-term memory. The third is reproduction, or the requirement that the child is able to replicate the behaviour (for instance, if they have the motor control to do so). The final element is motivation, which refers to the child having a reason to want to imitate their role model.

Children are most likely to continue producing this behaviour if it is reinforced, both directly and indirectly. Direct reinforcement would refer to the child receiving some benefit or reward for producing gender-appropriate behaviour or a punishment for gender-nonconforming behaviour, such as boys being encouraged to be active and assertive and scolded for crying. Indirect reinforcement, however, refers to the child observing the behaviour in someone else and seeing it benefit them or lead to negative consequences for them. For instance, if a girl sees another girl praised for looking pretty in dresses, she may decide she wants to wear dresses too in order to receive that praise. If she sees her role model express distaste for girls playing sports, she may decide not to show an interest in them.

**Q63** Distinguish between the social learning theory explanation of gender development and Freud's explanation. **[6 marks]**

Both the social learning theory and Freud's theory are in agreement that a key influence on a child's gender identity is the same-sex parent. However, the social learning theory is much more holistic and suggests that a wide range of gender-appropriate role models can shape a child's gender identity, while Freud is quite rigid in suggesting it is only the same-sex parent. Furthermore, the social learning theory would point to the conscious mediational processes in observing and reproducing a certain gendered behaviour, however Freud's theory mainly involves the unconscious mind through the Oedipus and Electra complexes.

Social learning theory also suggests that this modelling and learning is an ongoing process, while Freud's Oedipus and Electra complexes are said to occur only in the phallic stage of development. In a psychodynamic view, children are 'bisexual' (both masculine and feminine) before this stage and have fully completed developing their gender identity once their Oedipus or Electra complexes are resolved. This confines the development of gender identity and gendered behaviours to a specific stage, which social learning theory does not do.

**Q64** Give one strength of the social learning theory as applied to gender development. **[3 marks]**

One strength of the social learning theory is that there is research evidence to support it. In a classic study by Smith and Lloyd, a sample of babies were dressed half the time in boy's clothes and half the time in girl's clothes, irrespective of their actual gender. They found that when adults interacted with the babies, those that were assumed to be boys by the parents due to their clothing were given a hammer-shaped rattle and were encouraged to be adventurous and active. When those same babies were dressed as girls, the adults gave them a cuddly doll and they told the infants that they were 'pretty' multiple times. This suggests that gender appropriate behaviours are impressed upon children at a young age through differential reinforcement.

**Q65** Give two limitations of the social learning theory as applied to gender development. **[6 marks]**

One limitation of the social learning theory is that it could be argued it places too little emphasis on the influence of genes and chromosomes, only considering the role of the environment in the development of gender. For instance, in the case of David Reimer, the effort to get him to develop a female gender identity despite being genetically male failed. Many modern researchers now reject an explanation of gender that focuses on one aspect and rather adopt a more holisitic theory such as the biosocial or biopsychosocial theory, stating that both biology and social, or biological, psychological/cognitive, and social factors play a role. This can therefore account for both innate biological differences between boys and girls and the reinforcement of gender through cultural expectations and social interactions.

Furthermore, critics have also expressed concerns suggesting the social learning theory doesn't provide a sufficient explanation of how learning processes change with age. Firstly, there are some age limitations as children may struggle to reproduce behaviours if they aren't physically or intellectually capable of doing so. Furthermore, the understanding that modelling of gender-appropriate behaviour can oocur at any age may not be the case. This is because, although the child may take note of the behaviour of the same-sex role model from an early age, they are unlikely to imitate this gender-appropriate behaviour until much later, according to Dubin. This may point to Kolhberg's theory that children don't become active in their gender development until they reach gender constancy. Because this is not accounted for, social learning theory is arguably an incomplete explanation of gender development.

**Q66** Using a gender-related example, explain one reason why some adult behaviours or actions seen by children are not copied. **[2 marks]**

If there is a lack of identification between the child and the adult, then the child is less likely to observe and imitate the behaviour. For example, the boy may not see his mother as a role model because he sees her as different to him, so if he sees his mother cooking, he won't copy this behaviour as he may think it is for girls to cook.

**Q67** Describe one study that has the social learning theory as applied to gender development. **[4 marks]**

In a classic study by Smith and Lloyd, babies were dressed half the time in boy's clothes and half the time in girl's clothes, irrespective of their actual gender. They found that when adults interacted with the babies, those that were assumed to be boys by the parents due to their clothing were given a hammer-shaped rattle and were encouraged to be adventurous and active. When those same babies were dressed as girls, the adults gave them a cuddly doll and they told the infants that they were 'pretty' multiple times. This suggests that gender appropriate behaviours are impressed upon children at a young age through differential reinforcement.

# Application question

**Q68** Read the article below.

> **Is your child watching you?**
>
> Research by social learning theorists into gender development has shown that children learn many of their gender-related behaviours from others. There are many examples of children copying the behaviour of adults, such as a young girl trying on her mother's make-up. Of course, there are many reasons why some adult behaviours or actions seen by children are not copied.

Briefly explain what social learning theorists mean by modelling in relation to gender development. Refer to the article above in your answer. **[2 marks]**

Modelling is the process by which a child imitiates a gender-appropriate behaviour that has been exhibitied by their role model. In the article, it suggests that the young girl is modelling the behaviour of her mother (the role model) by trying on her make-up. The article also mentions that some behaviours and actions are not copied, which social learning theory can account for in multiple ways. For instance, the child may lack the physical ability to reproduce some behvaiours (e.g. by having insufficient fine motor skills), may not have paid adequate attention or adequately retained information, may not have enough motivation to copy a behaviour, or may not consider a specific adult to be their model.

# Essay questions

**Q69** Discuss the social learning theory as applied to gender development. **[16 marks]**

The social learning theory of gender development states that our gendered behaviour is learnt from observing others. It draws attention to the influence of nurture and the way our environment shapes gender development.

Before a child starts observing others, they will first undergo identification. This refers to the process by which a child 'attaches' themselves to a person who is seen to be 'like them' and who has qualities the child admires. These individuals are known as role models and they may be part of a child's immediate environment or present within media. Modelling is the precise demonstration of a behaviour that may be imitated by an observer, and this imitation occurs when a child identifies with a role model. For example, a mother may make dinner set the table (stereotypical behaviour) and her daughter will go on to imitate this in her play..

The process by which they observe and imitate this gendered behaviour is known as mediational processes. According to Bandura, there are four elements that lead to the behaviours taking place. The first is attention, in which the child observes and notices the behaviour of their role model. The second is retention, in which they code and store this knowledge into their long-term memory. The third is reproduction, or the requirement that the child is able to replicate the behaviour (for instance, if they have the motor control to do so). The final element is motivation, which refers to the child having a reason to want to imitate their role model.

Children are most likely to continue producing this behaviour if it is reinforced, both directly and indirectly. Direct reinforcement would refer to the child receiving some benefit or reward for producing gender-appropriate behaviour or a punishment for gender-nonconforming behaviour, such as boys being encouraged to be active and assertive and scolded for crying. Indirect reinforcement, however, refers to the child observing the behaviour in someone else and seeing it benefit them or lead to negative consequences for them. For instance, if a girl sees another girl praised for looking pretty in dresses, she may decide she wants to wear dresses too in order to receive that praise. If she sees her role model express distaste for girls playing sports, she may decide not to show an interest in them.

One strength of the social learning theory is that there is supporting research evidence. In a classic study by Smith and Lloyd, a sample of babies were dressed half the time in boy's clothes and half the time in girl's clothes, irrespective of their actual gender. They found that when adults interacted with the babies, those that were assumed to be boys by the parents due to their clothing were given a hammer-shaped rattle and were encouraged to be adventurous and active. When those same babies were dressed as girls, the adults gave them a cuddly doll and they told the infants that they were 'pretty' multiple times. This suggests that gender appropriate behaviours are impressed upon children at a young age through differential reinforcement.

One limitation of the social learning theory is that it could be argued it places too little emphasis on the influence of genes and chromosomes, only considering the role of the environment in the development of gender. For instance, in the case of David Reimer, the effort to get him to develop a female gender identity despite being genetically male failed. Many modern researchers now reject an explanation of gender that focuses on one aspect and rather accept a more holisitic theory such as the biosocial theory, stating that both biology and social, or biopsychosocial theory, which states that biological, psychological/cognitive, and social factors all play a role. This can therefore account for both innate biological differences between boys and girls and the reinforcement of gender through cultural expectations and social interactions.

Furthermore, critics have also expressed concerns suggesting the social learning theory doesn't provide a sufficient explanation of how learning processes change with age. Firstly, there are some age limitations as children may struggle to reproduce behaviours if they aren't physically or intellectually capable of doing so. Furthermore, the understanding that modelling of gender-appropriate behaviour can oocur at any age may not be the case. This is because, although the child may take note of the behaviour of the same-sex role model from an early age, they are unlikely to imitate this gender-appropriate behaviour until much later, according to Dubin. This may point to Kolhberg's theory that children don't become active in their gender development until they reach gender constancy. Because this is not accounted for, social learning theory is arguably an incomplete explanation of gender development.

**Q70** Discuss biological and social learning explanations of gender development. Refer to evidence in your answer. **[16 marks]**

One biological explanation for gender development is the influence of chromosomes and hormones. The sex of a baby is determined at conception when the sperm and ovum form a zygote (fertilised egg). The sperm and the egg both contribute chromosomes to the zygote. The 23rd chromosome pair contains DNA instructions to determine the zygote's sex. The ovum can only supply an X chromosome while the sperm can contribute either an X or a Y chromosome. If the sperm contributes a Y chromosome the zygote will be genetically male (XY), if the sperm contributes an X the zygote will be female (XX).

Hormones are chemical substances secreted by glands throughout the body and carried in the bloodstream. The same sex hormones occur in both men and women but differ in amounts and in the effect that they have upon different parts of the body. Important male hormones are called androgens, with testosterone being most widely known. Testosterone is a sex hormone which is more present in males than females and which affects development and behaviour both before and after birth. Testosterone, when released in the womb, causes the development of male sex organs at 8 weeks. During puberty, testosterone causes male secondary sex characteristics like facial hair to develop, as well as typically masculine behaviours such as aggression and a higher sex drive. For females, oestrogen governs the development of secondary sexual characteristics and menstruation, and in combination with oxytocin, is thought to contribute to feminine traits and behaviours.

Wang et al. researched the role of testosterone in gendered traits and behaviours through giving 227 hypogonadal men testosterone therapy for 180 days. Hypogonadism is a condition in which a man's testes fail to produce testosterone within normal ranges, so this allowed the researchers to isolate the effects of testosterone specifically. This therapy improved sexual function, libido and mood and increases muscle strength. This indicates that testosterone has a strong influence on male sexual arousal, as well as physical development.

However, the theory that both gender and sex are entirely biologically determined is in direct contrast to the social learning theory of gender development, which describes it as an entirely social process. It states that our gendered behaviour is learnt from observing others and draws attention to the influence of nurture where our environment shapes gender development.

Before a child starts observing others, they will first undergo identification. This refers to the process by which a child 'attaches' themselves to a person who is seen to be 'like them' and who has qualities the child admires. These individuals are known as role models and they may be part of a child's immediate environment or present within media. Modelling is the precise demonstration of a behaviour that may be imitated by an observer. For example, a mother may make dinner and set the table (stereotypical behaviour) and her daughter will go on to imitate this in her play.

The process by which they observe and imitate this gendered behaviour is known as mediational processes. According to Bandura, there are four elements that lead to the behaviours taking place. The first is attention, in which the child observes and notices the behaviour of their role model. The second is retention, in which they code and store this knowledge into their long-term memory. The third is reproduction, or the requirement that the child is able to replicate the behaviour (for instance, if they have the motor control to do so). The final element is motivation, which refers to the child having a reason to want to imitate their role model.

Children are most likely to continue producing this behaviour if it is reinforced, both directly and indirectly. Direct reinforcement would refer to the child receiving some benefit or reward for producing gender-appropriate behaviour or a punishment for gender-nonconforming behaviour, such as boys being encouraged to be active and assertive and scolded for crying. Indirect reinforcement, however, refers to the child observing the behaviour in someone else and seeing it benefit them or lead to negative consequences for them. For instance, if a girl sees another girl praised for looking pretty in dresses, she may decide she wants to wear dresses too in order to receive that praise. If she sees her role model express distaste for girls playing sports, she may decide not to show an interest in them.

There is research evidence to support this theory as well. Smith and Lloyd found that when adults interacted with babies, their behaviour depended on the gender which they perceived them to be based on their clothing. For instance, those that were assumed to be boys by the adults due to their clothing were given a hammer-shaped rattle and were encouraged to be adventurous and active. When those same babies were dressed as girls, the adults gave them a cuddly doll and they told the infants that they were 'pretty' multiple times. This suggests that gender appropriate behaviours are impressed upon children at a young age through differential reinforcement and do not occur naturally as they would if they were solely down to innate biology.

That said, as there is evidence for both elements, many modern researchers now reject an explanation of gender that focuses on one aspect and rather accept a more holisitic theory such as the biosocial theory, stating that both biology and social, or biopsychosocial theory, which states that biological, psychological/cognitive, and social factors all play a role. This can therefore account for both innate biological differences between boys and girls and the reinforcement of gender through cultural expectations and social interactions. We can see this in studies like the David Reimer case study, in which a biological male was raised socially as a girl but was unable to settle into a female identity despite the social reinforcement, and the existence of transgender people, who transition despite both biology and any attempts to socialise them into gender conformity as children. All of this suggest that gender is more complex than either of these examples currently adequately explain.

# Culture and media influences on gender development

## Short response questions

**Q71** Outline the influence of culture on gender roles. [6 marks]

Which elements of gender exist across all cultures and which vary are crucial as this helps psychologists to determine which may be an innate biological difference (nature) and which differences are socially created (nurture). Mead carried out a cross-cultural study of gender roles of three tribal groups on New Guinea Islands. The Arapesh were all considered gentle and responsive (similar to the Western conceptions of femininity). The Mundugumor were all considered hostile and aggressive (similar to the Western conceptions of masculinity). Finally, in the Tchambuli tribe, women were dominant and organised while the men were passive (the reverse of the Western norm). This suggests that there may not be a direct biological relationship between sex and gender roles and that it may be culturally determined. However, Buss found consistent similarities in mate preference in 37 countries across all continents: women sought men who could offer wealth and resources, while men sought women with youth and physical attractiveness. This suggests that some components of gender roles may be biological rather than cultural.

**Q72** Outline the influence of media on gender roles. [6 marks]

Just as children learn from and imitate role models in their individual lives, they also learn from and imitate role models in media. In both contexts, children are more likely to select role models who are the same sex as them and who produce gender-appropriate behaviour. Bussey and Bandura demonstrated that the media impress very clear and rigid gender stereotypes, where men are seen as ambitious and independent whilst women are seen as dependent and passive. Furthermore, Furnham and Farragher found that men were more likely to be portrayed as autonomous within professional contexts in the media, while women are often seen occupying familial setting. There is evidence to suggest that children with more exposure to media tend to display more gender-stereotypical ideas, views and behaviours. This suggests that these media portrayals provide additional models for children and reinforce traditional or mainstream gender roles, encouraging them to imitate these behaviours and internalise these attitudes.

**Q73** Give one strength into the influence of either culture or media on gender roles. **[3 marks]**

There is research evidence to suggest that both media and culture influence gender roles. Williams et al. had the rare opportunity to examine the effect of new media on a town in British Colombia who were about to receive a TV signal for the first time. The researchers carried out surveys to assess the behaviour and attitudes of the townsfolk before and after the introduction of TV. They also investigated a town with access to only one Canadian television channel, and one with multiple channels. They found that the introduction of television in the first town led to children developing a more rigid and sex-typed view of gender roles, and that the children in the town with multiple channels had more stereotypical ideas around gender than those with only one or who had only recently gained access to television. This suggests that both pre-existing cultural norms and media influences come together to influence gender roles and perceptions of them.

**Q74** Give two limitations into the influence of either culture or media on gender roles. **[6 marks]**

Although it is generally considered that the media has a strong impact and influence on the formation and maintenance of children's concepts of gender, it is difficult to establish cause and effect within these studies. The conventional explanation is that the media to a large degree is the cause of such stereotypical norms by portraying men and women in a particular way. However, it is just as likely that the media simply reflects the social norms about males and females rather than causing them. The large majority of children are regularly exposed to media from an early age and therefore control groups of children who aren't 'under the media's influence' aren't easily available as a control group. This makes it very difficult to establish causation, and therefore makes it very difficult to study in a scientifically valid way.

It is also important to note that most research covering the media's influence has focused on the effect of the media in reinforcing the status quo of gender stereotypes. However, more recently, there have been many examples of counter-stereotypes in the media which challenge traditional ideas of masculinity and femininity. For instance, though her appearance conforms to gender norms, the princess in the Disney film Brave shows a woman interested in weaponry and uninterested in marriage. Yet how children respond to these portrayals varies based on their own gender. Researchers found that gender stereotyping was reduced when women were in non-stereotypical roles, it was also found that pre-adolescent boys' stereotypes became stronger following exposure to non-traditional role models.

**Q75** Outline one study that has investigated the influence of culture on gender roles. **[6 marks]**

Mead carried out a cross-cultural study of gender roles of three tribal groups on New Guinea Islands. The Arapesh were all considered gentle and responsive (similar to the Western conceptions of femininity). The Mundugumor were all considered hostile and aggressive (similar to the Western conceptions of masculinity). Finally, in the Tchambuli tribe, women were dominant and organised while the men were passive (the reverse of the Western norm). This suggests that there may not be a direct biological relationship between sex and gender roles and that it may be culturally determined by the norms and values of an individual's culture.

**Q76** Outline one study that has investigated the influence of media on gender roles. **[6 marks]**

Williams et al. had the rare opportunity to examine the effect of new media on a town in British Colombia who were about to receive a TV signal for the first time. The researchers carried out surveys to assess the behaviour and attitudes of the townsfolk before and after the introduction of TV. They also investigated a town with access to only one Canadian television channel, and one with multiple channels. They found that the introduction of television in the first town led to children developing a more rigid and sex-typed view of gender roles, and that the children in the town with multiple channels had more stereotypical ideas around gender than those with only one or who had only recently gained access to television. This suggests that both pre-existing cultural norms and media influences come together to influence gender roles and perceptions of them.

# Essay questions

**Q77** Discuss research into the influence of culture and/or media on gender roles. **[16 marks]**

Which elements of gender exist across all cultures and which vary are crucial as this helps psychologists to determine which may be an innate biological difference (nature) and which differences are socially created (nurture). As different cultures will have different norms, priorities, traditions, and standards, they may have different ideas around gender and gendered behaviour.

For instance, Mead carried out a cross-cultural study of gender roles of three tribal groups on New Guinea Islands. The Arapesh were all considered gentle and responsive (similar to the Western conceptions of femininity). The Mundugumor were all considered hostile and aggressive (similar to the Western conceptions of masculinity). Finally, in the Tchambuli tribe, women were dominant and organised while the men were passive (the reverse of the Western norm). This suggests that there may not be a direct biological relationship between sex and gender roles and that it may be culturally determined. However, Buss found consistent similarities in mate preference in 37 countries across all continents: women sought men who could offer wealth and resources, while men sought women with youth and physical attractiveness. This suggests that some components of gender roles may be biological rather than cultural.

However, it is practically impossible to separate nature and nurture when it comes to the development of gender roles. This is because as soon as children are born – and arguably even before – gender role expectations are put on them. When we consider the impacts of both globalisation and colonialism on homogenising gender expectations globally, it becomes even more difficult to determine which behaviours are a result of nature and which are a result of nurture. Cultural differences have become less evident through both the world becoming more interconnected and the imposition of White Western norms onto colonised countries. Therefore, it becomes very difficult to determine where biological influences stop and social influence starts. An alternative explanation is that they both influence each other in the development of gender roles, as there is supporting evidence for both nature and nurture explanations.

One of the ways in which gender roles are communicated is through media. This, too, is becoming more international, with even non-Anglophone children accessing dubbed and subtitled versions of English-speaking media.

Just as children learn from and imitate role models in their individual lives, they also learn from and imitate role models in media. In both contexts, children are more likely to select role models who are the same sex as them and who produce gender-appropriate behaviour. Bussey and Bandura demonstrated that the media impress very clear and rigid gender stereotypes, where men are seen as ambitious and independent whilst women are seen as dependent and passive. Furthermore, Furnham and Farragher found that men were more likely to be portrayed as autonomous within professional contexts in the media, while women are often seen occupying familial setting. There is evidence from McGhee and Frueh to suggest that children with more exposure to media tend to display more gender-stereotypical ideas, views and behaviours. This suggests that these media portrayals provide additional models for children and reinforce traditional or mainstream gender roles, encouraging them to imitate these behaviours and internalise these attitudes.

However, this research can only show correlation and not causation. It is not possible to determine whether these portrayals in media result in more stereotypical ideas, behaviours, and views or whether they are reflecting the existing reality where those ideas, behaviours, and views already exist. It is likely that they both reinforce one another, meaning that media cannot be solely responsible for perceptions around gender roles.

That said, there has been research which was able to isolate the effect of media on gender roles. Williams et al. had the rare opportunity to examine the effect of new media on a town in British Colombia who were about to receive a TV signal for the first time, isolating a form of media's impact. The researchers carried out surveys to assess the behaviour and attitudes of the townsfolk before and after the introduction of TV. They also investigated a town with access to only one Canadian television channel, and one with multiple channels. They found that the introduction of television in the first town led to children developing a more rigid and sex-typed view of gender roles, and that the children in the town with multiple channels had more stereotypical ideas around gender than those with only one or who had only recently gained access to television. This suggests that both pre-existing cultural norms and media influences come together to influence gender roles and perceptions of them. However, the children in this town still had access to other forms of media, and it is impossible to fully control for this.

While this research still has relatively high validity due to being able to isolate the impact of television fairly well, it still does not consider the influences of other factors. Two children who engage with the same media can have vastly different attitudes towards gender and gender roles. This demonstrates that while media may have an impact, it is not the sole factor.

# Atypical gender development

## Key term questions

**Q78** Explain what is meant by gender identity disorder. **[3 marks]**

Gender identity disorder, also known as gender dysphoria, is characterised by strong, persistent feelings of identification with the opposite gender and discomfort with one's own assigned gender. It also is a serious source of stress and is recognised as a psychological disorder. People with gender dysphoria desire to live as members of the opposite sex and will typically dress and use mannerisms associated with the other gender. Many may also opt for to undergo surgeries to change their secondary sex characteristics and external genitalia to that of the desired sex.

## Short response questions

**Q79** Outline one or more social explanations for gender identity disorder. **[6 marks]**

One social-psychological explanation is the psychoanalytic theory. Ovesey and Person argued that gender dysphoria in biological males is caused by experiencing extreme separation anxiety before gender identity has been established. They believe that the child desires of a symbiotic fusion with their mother to relieve their anxiety and remove the danger of separation. The consequence of this is that the child becomes the mother and thus adopts a female gender identity. Stoller corroborates this and reports that when interviewing gender dysphoric biological males, they were seen to display overly close relationships to their mother, which he proposed led to a greater female identification and atypical gender identity in long-term.

Another social explanation is social learning theory. This theory proposes gender dysphoria is caused by children observing and imitating role models of the opposite sex. Ordinarily, children's role models are of the same sex as they are usually someone who they both perceive to be like them and as having desirable traits, but if all or most of these role models are of the opposite sex, they may learn and desire those behaviours. As with social learning of gender linked to biological sex, this can be reinforced directly or indirectly. For instance, if a boy sees his mother being complimented on her clothing, he may desire compliments and thus imitate her (indirect reinforcement). Equally, if a girl is told that she cannot do certain activities because of her gender, she may wish to be a boy in order to avoid punishment. In both of these cases, the reinforcement could result in gender identity disorder.

### Q80 Give one strength of a social explanation for gender identity disorder. [3 marks]

One strength of social explanation is that there is evidence to support it in the form of twin studies. Monozygotic (MZ) twins share 100% of their genetics, so if gender dysphoria was solely caused by biological factors, psychologists would expect to see both twins presenting with it. However, Diamond (2003) found that this was not the case. In genetically male MZ twin pairs where one was transgender, there was only a 33% chance that her twin would also experience gender dysphoria. In genetically female MZ pairs where one twin was transgender, there was a 23% chance his twin would also have gender dysphoria. This suggests that there is a strong social element, which social explanations can account for.

### Q81 Give two limitations of a social explanation for gender identity disorder. [6 marks]

One weakness of one social explanation is that the psychoanalytic theory particularly only applies to transgender women and doesn't provide a comprehensive account of gender dysphoria in transgender men. However, even for transgender women, research by Rekers suggests that gender dysphoria was more likely to occur with the absence of the father than with extreme separation anxiety from the mother. Furthermore the concept is difficult to test because the fantasies that centre on the mother occur on an unconscious level and those experiencing these fantasies may not even be aware of them. This is a weakness because it means it can't be scientifically tested, so there is no objective way to verify if the unconscious fantasy triggers gender identity disorder.

Another weakness of a social explanation is that the social learning theory does not fully explain what causes some children to select role models of the opposite sex and learn opposite sex behaviours. The theory states that children select role models who are like them, which typically requires them to be the same sex. But if they are already perceiving themselves as like someone of the opposite sex to the extent that this overrides traditional gender identity development, this suggests that they are already experiencing some form of gender dysphoria when selecting role models. This is a weakness because it means this theory only describes the effects of gender dysphoria and doesn't explain its possible origins.

### Q82 Outline one or more biological explanations for gender identity disorder. [6 marks]

One biological explanation for gender identity disorder is the brain sex theory. This suggests that gender dysphoria is caused by specific brain structures which are abnormal and thus incompatible with their assigned biological sex. Zhou et al. studied the bed nucleus of the stria terminalis (BSTc), which is usually it is 40% larger in males than females, in six male to female transgender cadavers compared to cisgender (non-transgender) male and cisgender female controls. In post-mortem examinations, the BSTc of transgender women was found to be much more similar to the cisgender female controls than the cisgender male controls. This suggests that transgender women have female brain structures. This was followed up by Kruijver et al., who studied the number of neurons in transgender women and found that they had an average BSTc neuron number in the female range.

Another biological explanation for gender identity disorder is prenatal hormones. While this cannot be scientifically studied as it is unethical to alter the prenatal hormones a foetus is exposed to and it can be difficult to measure them, there is still some research evidence to support it. Erickson-Schroth (2013) found that at least 5.2% of biological females with congenital adrenal hyperplasia, a condition which causes increased testosterone exposure in the womb, develop gender dysphoria. This is much higher than the average, which is less than 1%. This suggests that prenatal testosterone exposure increases the chances of biologically female people developing gender dysphoria.

**Q83** Give one strength of the biological explanation of gender identity disorder. **[3 marks]**

One strength of the biological explanation of gender identity disorder is that there is supporting evidence in the form of twin studies. If gender dysphoria is down to biological factors, the more similar two people are genetically, the more likely they are to share the condition. Beijsterveldt et al., Diamond, Heylens et al., and Coolidge et al. have all found much higher concordance rates between identical (monozygotic) twins than in non-identical (dizygotic) twins. While it is still not a 100% chance that if one monozygotic twin has gender dysphoria, the other will too, the fact that multiple studies find it increases the probability suggests a strong biological component. Because of this. Coolidge et al. estimated that gender dysphoria is 62% down to genetics and only 38% based on environmental experience. This shows that even when other factors are considered, biology is the most relevant.

**Q84** Give two limitations of the biological explanations of gender identity disorder. **[6 marks]**

One weakness of the brain sex theory is that there is evidence to contradict it. The BSTc is completely formed by age five so any hormone treatments that a transgender individual may undergo should not affect it. However Pol et al. found that hormone therapy can affect its size so these differences we observe may be due to the treatment of gender dysphoria rather than being a casue of it.

Another weakness of the biological explanation is that even the twin studies which provide support for the concept demonstrate that gender dysphoria is not entirely biological. Monozygotic (MZ) twins share 100% of their genetics, so if gender dysphoria was solely caused by biological factors, psychologists would expect to see both twins presenting with it in every case. However, Haylens et al. found that this only happens in 39% of cases. It is also worth considering that twins share a social environment for much of their upbringing, so even these numbers could be somewhat influenced by nurture factors. This demonstrates that genetics alone is unlikely to be the sole cause of gender dysphoria.

**Q85** Describe one study in which gender identity disorder was investigated. In your answer, explain what the researchers did and what they found. **[6 marks]**

One study that investigated gender identity disorder was Diamond (2013). He combined his own survey of transgender twins, where the twins were asked questions on gender and sexual practices, with a review of previously published studies on transgender twins. Amongst identical male and female twins where one experienced gender dysphoria, there were 33.3% and 22.8% chances respectively that their twin would also experiences. However, in contrast, the likelihood of both twins experiencing gender dysphoria among non-identical twins was only 2.6%. This higher likelihood for identical twins than non-identical twins highlights the strong genetic component to gender dysphoria. Furthermore, it also suggests that biological men are more prone to gender dysphoria than biological women.

# Essay questions

**Q86** Discuss biological and/or social explanations for gender identity disorder. Refer to evidence in your answer. **[16 marks]**

One social-psychological explanation is the psychoanalytic theory. Ovesey and Person argued that gender dysphoria in biological males is caused by experiencing extreme separation anxiety before gender identity has been established. They believe that the child desires of a symbiotic fusion with their mother to relieve their anxiety and remove the danger of separation. The consequence of this is that the child becomes the mother and thus adopts a female gender identity. Stoller corroborates this and reports that when interviewing gender dysphoric biological males, they were seen to display overly close relationships to their mother, which he proposed led to a greater female identification and atypical gender identity in long-term.

One weakness of this explanation is that only applies to transgender women and doesn't provide a comprehensive account of gender dysphoria in transgender men. However, even for transgender women, research by Rekers shows that gender dysphoria was more likely to occur with the absence of the father than extreme separation anxiety from the mother. Furthermore, the concept is difficult to test because the fantasies that centre on the mother occur on an unconscious level and those who are subject to these fantasies may not even be aware of them. This is a weakness because it means it can't be scientifically tested, so there is no objective way to verify this theory.

Another social explanation is the cognitive explanation proposed by Liben and Bigler, who extended the gender schema theory and suggested two pathways of gender development (dual pathway theory). The first pathway involves the development of gender schemas which then direct and influence gender-relevant attitudes and behaviours as part of 'normal development'. The second pathway suggests that the child's personal gender attitudes are affected by their own personal interests. For example, a boy who plays with dolls may believe playing with dolls is not gendered because they enjoy it, which would lead to more androgynous behaviour and a more flexible attitude to gender. However, this child could also begin identifying with more and more elements of their female gender schema, and then develop a female gender identity.

This theory, however, is more descriptive than comphrensive and explanatory. It does not explain how or why a child may become interested in activities that aren't relevant or appropriate to their own sex or what causes this to lead to more flexible gender schemas but still identifying with the birth sex in some children and to gender dysphoria in others. In this regard, biological factors may be what differentiates these children.

One biological explanation for gender identity disorder is the brain sex theory. This suggests that gender dysphoria is caused by specific brain structures which are abnormal and thus incompatible with their assigned biological sex. Zhou et al. studied the bed nucleus of the stria terminalis (BSTc), which is usually it is 40% larger in males than females, in six male to female transgender cadavers compared to cisgender (non-transgender) male and cisgender female controls. In post-mortem examinations, the BSTc of transgender women was found to be much more similar to the cisgender female controls than the cisgender male controls. This suggests that transgender women have female brain structures. This was followed up by Kruijver et al., who studied the number of neurons in transgender women and found that they had an average BSTc neuron number in the female range.

It is assumed that the BSTc is completely formed by age five so any hormone treatments that a transgender individual may undergo should not affect it. However, Pol et al. found that hormone therapy actually can affect its size, so these differences we observe may be due to the treatment of gender dysphoria rather than being a casue of it. In this case, the differences do not account for the cause of gender dysphoria, but instead provide evidence that medically transitioning changes multiple elements of a person's sex.

Another biological explanation for gender identity disorder is prenatal hormones. While this cannot be scientifically studied as it is unethical to alter the prenatal hormones a foetus is exposed to and it can be difficult to measure them, there is still some research evidence to support it. Erickson-Schroth (2013) found that at least 5.2% of biological females with congenital adrenal hyperplasia, a condition which causes increased testosterone exposure in the womb, develop gender dysphoria. This is much higher than the average, which is less than 1%. This suggests that prenatal testosterone exposure increases the chances of biologically female people developing gender dysphoria.

However, even the twin studies which provide support for the concept that gender dysphoria has a biological cause demonstrate that this is not the only factor. Monozygotic (MZ) twins share 100% of their genetics, so if gender dysphoria was solely caused by biological factors, psychologists would expect to see both twins presenting with it in every case. However, Haylens et al. found that this only happens in 39% of cases. It is also worth considering that twins share a social environment for much of their upbringing, so even these numbers could be somewhat influenced by nurture factors.

This demonstrates that genetics alone is unlikely to be the sole cause of gender dysphoria, and that it is likely a combination of factors. This theory is increasingly accepted, as researchers such as Coolidge et al. estimate that gender dysphoria is 62% caused by nature and 38% by nurture.

# Answers to identification questions

**Psychodynamic explanations of gender development**

**Q50**  A, D

**Q51**  C

# AQA Psychology
# Brilliant Model Answers

Are you aiming for the BEST grades possible? If you have answered yes, then look no further... these books are just what you need!

Written by experienced teachers and examiners, our series of books will allow you to learn, revise and organise your knowledge and understanding.

- ✓ Knowledge is precise and concise
- ✓ A well-structured and student friendly layout and organisation.
- ✓ Thorough and developed evaluation (the bit everyone needs extra help with).

## Psychologyzone series
psychologyzone.co.uk

## Sociologyzone series
sociologyzone.co.uk

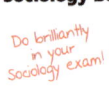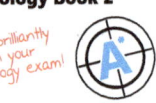
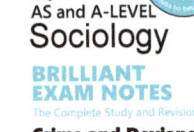

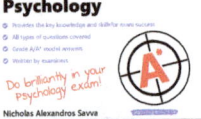
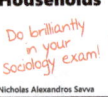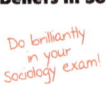

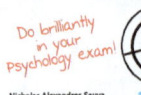
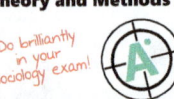

ISBN 978-1-906468-12-5

9 781906 468125

www.ingramcontent.com/pod-product-compliance
Lightning Source LLC
Chambersburg PA
CBHW080239040426
42333CB00045BA/2468